Mark's Argumentative Jesus

Mark's Argumentative Jesus

How Jesus Debated His Opponents
Using Greek Forms of Argumentation

Caurie Beaver

WIPF & STOCK · Eugene, Oregon

MARK'S ARGUMENTATIVE JESUS
How Jesus Debated His Opponents Using Greek Forms of Argumentation

Copyright © 2018 Caurie Beaver. All rights reserved. Except for brief quotations in critical publications or reviews, no part of this book may be reproduced in any manner without prior written permission from the publisher. Write: Permissions, Wipf and Stock Publishers, 199 W. 8th Ave., Suite 3, Eugene, OR 97401.

Wipf & Stock
An Imprint of Wipf and Stock Publishers
199 W. 8th Ave., Suite 3
Eugene, OR 97401

www.wipfandstock.com

PAPERBACK ISBN: 978-1-5326-4643-0
HARDCOVER ISBN: 978-1-5326-4644-7
EBOOK ISBN: 978-1-5326-4645-4

Manufactured in the U.S.A.

Once again, I gladly dedicate this book to my wife Sandra, who has dedicated, not a book, but her life to me, our daughter Kristen, and our two wonderful grandkids, Angelo and Mya.

Contents

Preface | ix
Acknowledgments | xi

	Introduction	1
I	The Beginning: Why Mark Has No Birth Story of Jesus	18
II	Arché: Why the First Word of Mark was Mistranslated As "Beginning"	25
III	What Difference Does it Make?	37
IV	Mark's "Simple" Rhetorical Arguments: The "for"(gar) Enthymemes	49
V	Complex Rhetorical Arguments: Mark's Account of Jesus' Debates	70
VI	The Enthymeme or Rhetorical Syllogism that Generated Mark's Persuasive Speech	102
VII	Elijah Must Come First: The Role of Elijah in Mark's Gospel	111
VIII	The Logos Must Come First: The Role of John "the Baptist" in John's Gospel	116
IX	Conclusion	128

Preface

AFTER I WROTE MY book, *Mark: A Twice-Told Tale*, I added Appendix I, "The Messiah: God's Son, Not David's," which dealt with Mark's use of a Hellenistic form of rhetorical argument frequently found in speeches at the time. Then I discovered that the first word of Mark, arché, was mistranslated as "beginning," instead of "guiding principle." This led to my writing Appendix II, "The Guiding Principle of Mark's Gospel: Elijah Must Come First," in which I argued that Mark was not primarily a story but a persuasive, argumentative discourse or speech, which could be expected to utilize a wide range of Hellenistic rhetorical devices.

Of course, Mark contained stories, but they were not told for their own sake, but for the sake of argument. However, when Mark told a story, we can analyze it as a story, but when he made an argument, or had Jesus make one, we must analyze it as one taking into account his reasoning and noting his conclusion. As light can be viewed as both particle and wave, the Gospel of Mark can be analyzed as both story and argumentative discourse. In *Mark: A Twice-Told Tale*, I explained how Mark told the story of Jesus; in the present book, I explain how Mark constructed an argument for Jesus' Messiahship, and also provided arguments for the argumentative Jesus.

Aristotle defined rhetoric as ". . . an ability, in each particular case, to see the available means of persuasion."[1] Whether a speech

---

1. *Aristotle: A Theory of Civic Discourse on Rhetoric*, Newly Translated, with Introduction, Notes, and Appendices by George A. Kennedy, (New York, Oxford University Press, 1991), p.14.

was convincing or not depended on three things: the ethos or character of the speaker (can the audience trust him or her), the pathos or receptivity of the audience (can the audience relate to the speaker), and finally, the logos or logic of the speaker's reasoning (does the audience find the speaker's arguments reasonable and convincing). As George Kennedy put it, the persuasiveness of a speech

> depends on three things: the truth and logical validity of what is being argued; the speaker's success in conveying to the audience the perception that he or she can be trusted; and the emotions that a speaker is able to awaken in an audience to accept the views advanced and act in accordance with them.[2]

Aristotle, the heir to early Greek rationalism, considered the logos or logical argument the most important means of persuasion.[3]

We know nothing about Mark's character (ethos) except what we can infer from the gospel itself, and the same is true of the probable response of his audience (pathos). However, we do have direct access to his argument (logos) and the variety of rhetorical forms in which he presented his case. All the talk about his fast paced narrative that would appeal to the practical Roman character must be balanced by a veritable profusion of Greek forms of rhetorical argumentation with which Mark appealed to the Hellenistic temper.

---

2. Ibid., p. ix.

3. John Herman Randall Jr., *Aristotle* (New York: Columbia University Press, 1960), p. 12. See also Albert Schweitzer's *Out of My Life and Thought*, translated by C. T. Campion, (New York: Henry Holt and Company, Twelfth Printing, 1959), p. 118.

Acknowledgments

I WISH TO EXPRESS my gratitude to the following persons:

Gerlof Homan, who taught me historical method at Central State College (now the University of Central Oklahoma) in Edmond, Oklahoma.

James M. Robinson, past Director of the Institute for Antiquity and Christianity in Claremont California, whose influence on my work is undeniable and acknowledged by him. He read my first book, *Mark: A Twice-Told Tale* in manuscript and praised it highly. He even said that his own work supported mine "importantly."

Althea Spencer-Miller of Scripps College in Claremont, California and her friend, who typed the manuscript to my first book, and said they stayed up all night reading it. Althea now teaches at Drew University.

Rev. Ann Schranz, minister of the Unitarian Universalist Congregation in Montclair, California, who read my book and understood the direction it was taking in Appendix II. Her generosity extended to interviewing me before her congregation after I had made two presentations to an adult group there led by Harry Ragland, whose lively members challenged me and made me feel welcome.

Norman Goldberg, my last supervisor at L.A. County Adult Protective Services, and his wife, Roberta, for their tireless efforts in acquiring books for me from the Internet.

Tom DeDobay, Music Professor at Chaffey College in Cucamonga, California, John Hendricks and Spencer Crump, L.A.

Co. Social Workers, whose friendly criticisms and occasional proddings were a continual source of inspiration to me, also merit special mention.

John Wipf, owner of Archives Bookstore in Pasadena, CA, and co-owner of Wipf and Stock Publishing Company in Eugene, OR, and to Jon Stock, his partner. Special thanks is due to Kristen Bareman Brack, John Wipf's niece, whose illustration of my first book showed she understood its two-fold theme and expressed it in a way that was truly brilliant. Nor can I fail to mention James Stock who informed me that Wipf and Stock would not only publish my book, but also include Appendix II, which has led to the present book.

Joanne Green of the Monclair Unitarian church who typed part of the manuscript and made some helpful suggestions.

My wife, Sandra, whose patient indulgence through many years of research created a deeply personal debt that I could never fully repay.

There are many others, whose relevance to the present work is more remote. I happily recognize the assistance of all of these teachers and friends without implicating them in its shortcomings.

Finally, Jana Wipf for her exceptional work of typing and arranging the manuscript for submission. Her efforts far exceeded my expectations, and I owe her an immense debt of gratitude.

Introduction

The Stories in Arguments

IF ACCORDING TO PSYCHOLOGIST, Pierre Janet, normal human memory takes the form of a story, which includes beliefs and feelings as well as facts, it would seem to follow that the remembered events were also originally experienced as a story as well.[1] In their book, *Arguments and Arguing*, Thomas A. Hollihan and Kevin T. Baaske held, "that all argument is story."[2] The philosophical basis of this viewpoint was worked out by Walter R. Fisher in his book *Human Communication as Narration: Toward a Philosophy of Reason, Value, and Action*. Concerning argument as story, he wrote,

> No matter how strictly a case is argued—scientifically, philosophically, or legally—it will always be a story, an interpretation of some aspect of the world that is historically and culturally grounded and shaped by human personality. Even the most well-argued case will be informed by other individuated forms besides argument, especially metaphor.[3]

---

1. Judith Hermann, *Trauma and Recovery*, (New York: Basic Books, A Division of HarperCollins Publishers, 1992), p. 175.

2. Thomas A. Hollihan and Kevin T. Baaske, *Argument and Arguing* (Prospect Heights, Illinois, 1994), p. 43.

3. Walter R. Fisher, *Human Communication As Narration: Toward a Philosophy of Reason, Value, and Action*, Columbia, South Carolina: University of South Carolina Press, 1987, 1989), p. 49.

In Fisher's narrative paradigm, argumentation appears as a form of storytelling. For example, we call that most argumentative setting imaginable, a trial, courtroom drama, in which a prosecutor tells a defendant's story to prove that he or she is guilty, and the defense attorney tells his client's story to show he is not guilty. In a political campaign, an equally argumentative context, newsmen and candidates both talk about establishing or changing a narrative or story. To use a story as an argument is not just an accommodation to the multitude that is deemed incapable of following a complex argument using formal logic. Ultimately, we all evaluate arguments as stories and estimate their probability and consistency with our own experience.

These observations are also borne out by a popular maxim that asserts that every story has two sides, for a two-sided story is an argument. By referring to a story as two-sided instead of two stories, folk wisdom recognizes the common ground in stories that forms the basis for argumentation.[4] If a story were demonstrated to an irrefutable certainty, it would have had only one side, leaving no room for argument. If, on the other hand, there were two entirely different stories, no common ground would exist to form the basis for argumentation. The two storytellers would simply be talking past one another with no possibility of a real engagement.

The Common Story: A Basis for Argumentation

In what follows, I will often concentrate on the differences between Jesus and his opponents; but first I will focus on their commonalities that permit them to engage in argumentation in

---

4. Vernon K. Robbins, *Jesus the Teacher*, (Minneapolis: Fortress Press, 2009) p. 6, previously published by Augsburg Fortress Press, 1984, 1992), See also C. H. Perelman and L. Olbrechts-Tyteca, *The New Rhetoric, A Treatise on Argumentation*, Translated by John Wilkinson and Purcell Weaver Center for the Study of Democratic Institutions, (Notre Dame Press, 1971), p. 1. "The domain of argumentation is that of the credible, the plausible, the probable, to the degree that the latter eludes certainty of calculations." Originally published as *La Nouvelle Rhétorique: Traité de l'Argumentation* Presses Universitaires de France, 1958.

INTRODUCTION

the first place—in other words, their common story. Before Rome destroyed Jerusalem in 70 CE, the Temple State held the various "sects" or factions together. On some things they agreed, on others disagreed, but the Torah and other shared traditions formed the common ground for their disputes as they shaped and directed the way(s) of life for the Jewish people. Of course, each sect claimed to possess the authentic traditions or represent the true Israel, but they defended their claims by appealing to the same Law of Moses and the prophets, which together was the law of the land.

Jesus and his opponents agreed on enough things to sustain an ongoing argument. This underlying agreement is best illustrated by the question as to which is the first commandment. A scribe overheard Jesus arguing with the Sadducees about the resurrection:

> And seeing that he answered them well, he asked him, "Which commandment is the first of all?" Jesus answered, "The first is, 'Hear, O Israel: the Lord our God, the Lord is one; you shall love the Lord your God with all your heart, and with all your soul, and with all your mind, and with all your strength.' The second is this, 'You shall love your neighbor as yourself.'" (Deut. 6:45, Mk. 12:29–31).

The scribe approved of Jesus' answer, and even repeated it almost word-for-word. Then he directed a jibe at the Sadducees, whom Jesus had just bested in the preceding debate, "this is much more important than all whole burnt offerings and sacrifices" (Mk. 12:33). These particular religious activities were, of course, the sacred occupation of the Sadducees, the priests of the Temple. Jesus, who was closer to the Pharisees on this issue, said to the scribe, "you are not far from the Kingdom of God" (Mk. 42:34).

Although the scribe with Jesus' silent consent pitted the love commandment against the sacrifices of the Temple, Jesus did not completely reject the latter. When he "healed" the leper, he enjoined him to make the offering that Moses commanded. It was in the area of belief about the resurrection that he parted company with the Sadducees. Even here, both appealed to the law of Moses as the foundation of their argument: the Sadducees to the Levirate marriage law (Gen. 38:8-11) and Jesus to the Burning Bush story (Deut. 25:5-10).

However, in the argument about divorce Jesus rejected Moses's provision for granting a bill of divorcement saying that Moses had only *permitted* not *commanded* it due to the hardness of the people's hearts. Here, Jesus appealed from Moses to the principle of creation saying that in the beginning (arché) it was not so.

The controversy about the resurrection resulted from the influx of beliefs about the afterlife, probably of Iranian Zoroastrian origin later modified by Greek notions. The Old Testament does not contain a definite belief in the resurrection, so its eschatological benefits were only for the final generation.[5] Along with the belief in the resurrection came belief in angels and demons. The books of Enoch and Daniel are witnesses to the beginnings of this infusion of ideas that later became a torrent. The Pharisees, who presumably originated among the pious Hasidim during the Maccabean revolt, accepted these new ideas while the Sadducees rejected them.[6]

On the question of whose son the Messiah would be, Mark/Jesus also parted company with the Pharisees, who held to the notion that the ruler of the End time would be a descendant of the royal house of David. However, the Davidic dynasty came to an end during or shortly after the Exile. For some groups, represented by the books of Daniel and Mark, the search for a replacement came to focus on a mysterious figure originating in the new eschatology, the Son of Man. For other groups, the power vacuum came to be filled by priests: the Maccabean revolt was initiated by priests, the Dead Sea Sect looked for a Messiah of both royal and priestly descent,[7] and finally the book of Hebrews called Jesus a High Priest (Heb. 4:14). Under the impact of Greek ideas, the

---

5. D. S. Russell, *The Method and Message of Jewish Apocalyptic*, (Philadelphia: The Westminster Press, 1964) p. 264f.

6. Ibid., p. 24.

7. James C. Vanderkam, *The Dead Sea Scrolls Today*, (Grand Rapids, Michigan/Cambridge, U.K.: William B. Eerdmans Publishing Company, 2010), p. 215.

INTRODUCTION

Messiah was also considered the Son of God. True, it has not gone unnoticed that some Israeli rulers were called God's son, which may in some cases only serve to date the source in question to Hellenistic times (Ps. 2:7).

Whatever their origin, these several titles available for the Messiah made for controversy as to whose son the Messiah was at the time of Jesus and Mark. According to Paul, a Pharisee, the Messiah was both a descendant of David and the Son of God:

> Paul, a servant of Jesus Christ, called to be an apostle, set apart for . . . the gospel concerning his Son, who was descended from David according to the flesh and was declared to be the Son of God with power according to the spirit of holiness by resurrection from the dead (Rom. 1:1–4).

The common basis for argumentation here is a Psalm of David, in which David supposedly called the Messiah his Lord (Ps. 110:1, Mk. 12:35–37), to which Jesus appealed to make his case that the messiah was not David's son, but David's Lord.

In the story about Satan casting out Satan, it is obvious that Jesus and his opponents shared a belief in Satan and demons, which provided common ground for argumentation. The only question was whose power Jesus used—Satan's or God's. Like Jesus' opponents, Jesus' own disciples questioned whose power a freelance exorcist used to cast out demons:

> John said to him [Jesus], "Teacher, we saw someone casting out demons in your name, and we tried to stop him, because he was not following us." But Jesus said, "do not stop him; for no one who does a deed of power in my name will be able soon afterward to speak evil of me. Whoever is not against us is for us" (Mk. 9:38–40).

Whereas this exorcist used the name of Jesus to cast out demons, Jesus was accused of using the ruler of demons to cast them out. However, in that case Satan would be working against himself, an unlikely scenario. In the argument that followed, Jesus took full advantage of this paradoxical situation.

Jesus even agreed with his opponents as to the obligation to pay taxes to Caesar in order to preserve their temple state, which, incidentally, also maintained his opponent's power base. But he called their attention to their equal obligation to grant God his due. In the revolt against Rome, this consensus was broken by the Zealots, whose leaders swore allegiance to God alone thereby incurring the wrath of Rome and the ultimate destruction of Jerusalem and the Temple State.

Finally, in the structural argument that generated Mark's persuasive discourse the common ground between Jesus and his opponents is even more obvious. Jesus agreed with the scribes who said that Elijah must come first before the Messiah appears. The disagreement centered on the question as to whether Elijah had already come (Jesus' claim) or was still to come (the scribes' claim). Mark/Jesus argued that John the Baptist was Elijah, but throughout the gospel both the people and their leaders rejected the notion that John the Baptist was Elijah, which also constituted a denial that Jesus was the Messiah.

The Arguments in Stories

The maxim asserting that there are two sides to every story appears to imply that all stories have an argumentative aspect. But what about stories that simply aim to entertain, inspire, or teach? Where is the argumentative element in such stories? The first two types of rhetoric—judicial and deliberative—call for decision or action, but the third type—epideictic, or ceremonial, rhetoric—appears to simply reinforce or celebrate the values already held by the community with no apparent goal of immediate action. However, to the extent that such rhetoric serves to increase the audience's adherence to commonly held values, it tends to increase the likelihood of decision or action when the occasion for it arises. Therefore, such rhetoric forms an integral part of argumentation itself by putting the audience in the proper frame of mind, disposing them to action.

Introduction

It is in this perspective that epideictic oratory has significance and importance for argumentation, because it strengthens the disposition toward action by increasing adherence to the values it lauds.[8]

In his book, *Understanding the Book of Hebrews: The Story Behind the Sermon*, Kenneth Schenck reconstructed the story behind the book of Hebrews' elaborate argumentative structure. As he put it,

> In reality I prefer the phrase "rhetorical world" to "thought world." By rhetorical world I refer to the story world of Hebrews in combination with the rhetoric that proceeds from it. Thus, while a gospel is a "story as discoursed" in narrative, Paul's letters and Hebrews are "stories as discoursed" in rhetoric.[9]

In my opinion, in the case of Hebrews, the story is embedded in the argument, while in the case of the Gospel of Mark the argument is immersed in and expressed through the story. Mark's gospel is just as argumentative as Hebrews, but in Mark the characters in the story carry much of the argument; whereas in Hebrews, the author makes the argument up front in which case it is apparent that the stories are subordinated to the argumentative discourse. If the first word of Mark had not been mistranslated, it would have been equally obvious that the stories in Mark were wedded to the argumentative purpose of the gospel. In a narrative genre, such as a history, biography or a novel, the argument is usually subordinated to the story, but in a discursive genre, such as a speech, lecture, or essay, the story is subordinated to the argument.

With the advent of the war between Rome and Judea, the narrative changed. After the destruction of the Temple, the surviving sects drifted apart, leaving the "common ground" for community building and argumentation a "no man's land." As the "consensus" fell apart the "law of the land" (the Torah) became the rule of two

---

8. C. H. Perelman and L. Olbrechts-Tyteca, *The New Rhetoric*, p. 50.

9. Kenneth Schenck, *Understanding the Book of Hebrews, The Story Behind the Sermon*, (Louisville, London: Westminster John Knox Press, 2003), p. 111 n. 9.

respective communities: the one led by the Pharisees and the other by Jesus' followers. The Pharisees claimed the exclusive right to interpret the Torah and developed into Formative Judaism, and Jesus' community interpreted the Law of Moses through the teachings of Jesus Christ, and it became Messianic Judaism.[10] It was only with the Gospel of Matthew that this split became clear. In Mark, Jesus told the leper he healed, "go show yourself to the priest, and offer for your cleansing *what Moses commanded*, as a testimony to them" (Mk. 1:44). In Matthew, Jesus said, "Go therefore and make disciples of all nations . . . teaching them to obey *everything that I have commanded you*" (Matt. 28:19–20).

As the church found in Jesus the Son of God, and even God himself, lost in all of this was Mark's image of a simple remarkable teacher, who taught with stories about ordinary people and common problems. He respected his opponents enough to argue with them, giving reasons for his teachings and not simply asserting them dogmatically. Mark's argumentative Jesus resembles in some respects the Gnostic's "living Jesus;" the context, of course, was different. Concerning this "living Jesus," Elaine Pagels wrote,

> Many of these secret writings, as we've seen, picture "the living Jesus" inviting questions, inquiry, and discussions about meaning—unlike Tertullian when he complains that "questions make people heretics" and demands that his hearers stop asking questions and simply accept the "rule of faith." And unlike those who insist that they already have all the answers they'll ever need, these sources invite us to recognize our own truths, to find our own voice, and to seek revelation not only past, but ongoing.[11]

When I read this statement, I remembered that Mark's Jesus asked a plethora of questions, over 100, which invites us to ask questions of our own. Mark's Jesus questioned his traditions

---

10. D. S. Russell, *The Method and Message of Apocalyptic*, pp. 20ff.; G. D. Kilpatrick, *The Origins of the Gospel According to St. Matthew*, (Oxford: At the Clarendon Press, 1950), p. 101.

11. Elaine Pagels, *Revelation: Visions, Prophecy, and Politics in the Book of Revelation*, (New York: Viking, 2012), pp. 176, 177. A raw count of questions in Mark places the number at over 100.

and common story, teaching us to question our own tradition, by which we can hope to reach common ground for community building, argumentative interaction to replace the global wars we are currently fighting.

Mark's Gospel as a Persuasive Speech

Did Mark's Jesus—in the words of George Kennedy, an expert in ancient rhetoric—use "sacred language" to assert "absolute claims of authoritative truth without evidence or logical argument?"[12] Or did he advance his claims by using the rhetorical arguments provided by his Hellenistic surroundings? Mark said that Jesus taught with authority and not as the scribes. Did he perhaps teach like the Greeks, who were famous for their dialectical and rhetorical skills at argumentation? After all, Kennedy knew that Greek language and culture had been penetrating the Near East for some three hundred years by the time of Jesus,[13] and Mark wrote his gospel in the Greek language. Anyone writing a persuasive speech in Greek at that time could hardly avoid using Greek rhetorical forms of argumentation. According to Mary Ann Tolbert, "well before the first century CE education in rhetoric was a basic part of the training of anyone who learned to write or read in the Greek language.[14]

Kennedy drew too sharp a distinction between the rhetoric of Greece and Rome, which developed in legal, political, and ceremonial settings, and the "sacred language" of the New Testament, which flourished in a religious context. According to Kennedy, the former was characterized by rational persuasion and the latter by authoritative proclamation. He flatly stated, "Jesus's message was

12. George A. Kennedy, *New Testament Interpretation through Rhetorical Criticism* (Chapel Hill: University of North Carolina Press, 1984), p. 104.
13. Ibid., p. 8.
14. Mary Ann Tolbert, "The Gospel of Mark," in the *New Testament Today*, ed. by Mark Allen Powell, (Louisville, Kentucky: Westminster John Knox Press, 1999), p. 51. Michael Stone in his book, *Scriptures, Sects and Visions: A Profile of Judaism from Ezra to the Jewish Revolts* (Philadelphia: Fortress Press, 1980) p. 95, puts it this way, "What is clear is that there was a penetration of Greek language and elements of Greek culture which was really quite considerable."

essentially proclaimed, not argued on the basis of probability and that is why it is often called by the Greek word for proclamation, Kerygma."[15] Then he conceded that often in the Old Testament, "something is added which seems to give a reason why the proclamation should be received and thus appeals at least in part to human rationality."[16]

This is clear from, "the first commandment: 'I am the Lord your God;" the evidence, 'who brought you out of the land of Egypt. . .'; therefore, 'You shall have no other gods before me." (Exo. 20:2–3) Kennedy added, "In classical rhetoric such a statement with a supporting reason is called an enthymeme.[17] Although he found such rhetorical arguments in the New Testament, he claimed that the Gospel of Mark used "sacred language" to proclaim its doctrine, and did not utilize rational arguments to any great extent.

I will soon demonstrate that Mark is literally saturated with such rhetorical arguments as enthymemes. Many books on Mark call attention to the gospel's frequent use of the word *euthus* (immediately) some 40 times and point out that it illustrates the rapid pace of the narrative.[18] Fewer books on the gospel evince an aware-

15. George A. Kennedy, *New Testament Interpretation through Rhetorical Criticism*, p. 6. By far the best critique of Kennedy's notion of radical Christian rhetoric is that of John R. Levison, essay entitled "Did the Spirit Inspire Rhetoric? An Exploration of George Kennedy's Definition of Early Christian Rhetoric" published in *Persuasive Artistry: Studies in New Testament Rhetoric in Honor of George A. Kennedy*, Edited by Duane F. Watson, (Sheffield, England: Academic Press, 1991), pp. 25–40. While Levison dealt with Kennedy's definition of early Christian Rhetoric, I critiqued Kennedy's denial of the prominence of rational argumentation in the Gospel of Mark.

16. George A. Kennedy, *New Testament Interpretation through Rhetorical Criticism*, p. 7.

17. Ibid., p. 7.

18. Caurie Beaver, *Mark: A Twice-Told Tale*, (Eugene, OR: Wipf and Stock, 2009), p. 83, previously published by Xlibris Corp., 2004. In that book, I speculated that Mark's introduction was linked to the body of the gospel by ". . .a terminological, continuation of the Greek word for 'straight' in the frequently used Markan expression 'straightway.' In Greek these two words are related much like their English counterparts (straight and straightway)" which is obscured by the current translation of straightway as "immediately." My views in

INTRODUCTION

ness of Mark's even more frequent use of the word *gar* (for) over 60 times, which by giving a reason for a preceding statement contributes to the pace of the argument.

Kennedy failed to notice the pervasiveness of Hellenistic forms of rhetorical argumentation in Mark because he probably thought that Mark considered Jesus the Son of God during his lifetime. In that case, when Jesus debated his opponents, there was no real contest, since there was never any danger that he would lose the argument. When we think about most popular descriptions of Jesus, the word argumentative does not readily come to mind. It might be allowed that he debated his opponents, but the outcome was never in doubt. He simply vanquished his enemies, leaving bystanders astonished. If his disciples misunderstood him, he rebuked them, as he did Peter who objected to his teaching about his impending death (Mk. 8:31–33), or taught them privately the true meaning of his public teachings (Mk. 4:10).

The focus was usually on the conclusion instead of the process of reasoning that led to the result. We will soon show that Mark's Jesus took into account the bases of his opponents' reasonings and addressed them with matching arguments. We will also demonstrate that Mark's Jesus was every bit as contentious and argumentative as the Apostle Paul, who used every rhetorical trick in the books to get his message across, becoming "all things to all people, that I might by all means save some" (1 Cor. 9:22).

---

this regard are confirmed by similar comments by Antoinette Clark Wire in her book, *The Case for Mark Composed in Performance*, Cascade Books, (Eugene, OR: Wipf and Stock, 2011), p. 83. Her notion that Mark was composed in oral presentations may also support my view that Mark is an argumentative discourse or persuasive speech.; Richard B. Vinson wrote an article entitled "A Comparative Study of the Use of Enthymemes in the Synoptic Gospels" published in Persuasive Artistry, Edited by Duane F. Watson. Pp. 118–141. His count of enthymemes in Mark, 77, differed from mine, over 60, is due to his inclusion of *hoti* enthymemes, while I dealt only with (*gar*) enthymemes. See p. 119. He also claimed that "No one would suggest that the gospel writers built their rhetorical or narrative strategies around enthymemes. . ." p. 131. In my opinion Mark did just that: both *hoti* and *gar* are casual particles that mean for or because.

In contrast to the usual view of Jesus, I will argue that Mark did not consider Jesus the Son of God during his lifetime, which permitted him to describe Jesus as a teacher who engaged in debates with various opponents. If Mark's Jesus simply proclaimed his message, as Kennedy said he did, one could merely accept it by faith or reject it, but one could not debate with it. However, if Mark's Jesus argued his case, one would be obliged to consider his premises, estimate the strength of his argument, and even entertain alternatives to his conclusions.

Mark as a Teacher in Antioch

While Jesus' debates are described as taking place in various public and private settings, the Gospel of Mark itself probably originated in an educational context. In view of all the exalted titles that have gathered around Jesus, it is remarkable that Mark portrayed him as a teacher, using words related to teacher and teaching almost 30 times. (Mk. 1:21–22, 27; 5:35; 6:2, 25, 30, 34; 8:31; 9:17, 31, 38; 10:1, 17, 20, 35; 11:17, 18; 12:14, 19, 32, 35, 38; 13:1; 14:14, 45, and 49). When he described Jesus as a teacher, Mark also drew a self-portrait. We will shortly give a reason to believe that the school or synagogue where Mark taught was located in Antioch where Matthew succeeded him in the role of a teacher. Jesus may also have been a teacher, but Mark's portrayal of Jesus' role as one is Mark's own, and cannot with assurance be attributed to Jesus himself.

Krister Stendahl claimed that the Gospel of Matthew also originated in an educational setting. After describing how Matthew arrived at his portrait of Jesus, Stendahl wrote, "this together with the structure of the gospel, gave me some reason to speak of a School of St. Matthew, not the School of Jesus.[19] Here, Stendahl is withdrawing only that part of a statement which referred to the "School of Jesus." With this retraction in mind, his statement merits serious consideration. Therefore, I will quote him in full.

---

19. Krister Stendahl, *The School of St. Matthew* (Ramsey, New Jersey, Sigler Press, 1991), p. x.

INTRODUCTION

There may therefore be an unbroken line from the School of Jesus via the "teaching of the Apostles," the "ways" of Paul, the basic teaching of Mark and other *servants of the word*, and the more mature School of John to the rather elaborate School of Matthew with its ingenious interpretation of the O.T. as the crown of its scholarship.[20]

When B. Gerhardsson, author of *Memory and Manuscript*, appealed to Stendahl's "School of Jesus" to support his own peculiar theory about the transmission of the gospel tradition, Stendahl realized that he had overstated the case. While he no longer spoke about the School of Jesus, Stendahl still stood by his theory about the School of St. Matthew. He could have added "the school of Mark," but not Jesus.

However, by far the most interesting thing about this quotation is the reference to "the basic teaching of Mark," which forms a parallel to Hebrews 5:12 and 6:1, "the basic teaching about Christ." It is not certain that Stendahl had in mind the first line of Mark, but it would have been accurate if he had. It is even plausible , if not probable, that Hebrews 5:12 and 6:1 are paraphrases of Mark 1:1. In Greek, the form of the three statements is much closer than it is in translation. The notion that we have to do with a paraphrase of Mark 1:1 is also suggested by the way Hebrews repeated the statement in the same form as if he were following the wording of a source.

Allen Wikgren, one of the editors of the Nestle Aland Greek New Testament expressed a very similar view in the course of which he defined the first word of Mark, arché, as "first thing," in the sense of "rudiments" or "elements" or "essentials" of the gospel.[21] This elementary instruction led on to the more advanced teaching in Hebrews. While it was probably not Mark's view of the gospel, it does appear to have been the view of Mark held by Matthew, Hebrews, and possibly John. Mark's own view of his gospel was that it contained both the elementary teaching (in parables)

---

20. Ibid., pp. 33, 34.
21. Allen Wikgren, "ΑΡΧΗ ΤΟΥ ΕΥΑΓΓΕΛΙΟΥ," *Journal of Biblical Literature*, 61 (1942), p. 17.

and the deeper message (interpretation), which could only be understood by those who had ears to hear.

The Modern Theological Context of Gospel Studies: The Origin of the Gospels in Missionary Preaching

To understand how a scholar with the stature of George Kennedy, an expert in rhetoric, failed to see the prominence of argumentative forms in Mark, the clues to which his expertise is designed to detect, requires an exceptional explanation. The cause is to be found in his acceptance of the proclamation (preaching) theology of Rudolph Bultmann, whose remarkable career dominated German critical theology in the twentieth century.[22] Anyone who doubts the accuracy of this characterization merely needs to read the Foreword to Norman Perrin's book, *The Promise of Bultmann*, in which Nancy Perrin wrote,

> He (Perrin) considered Bultmann to be the greatest New Testament scholar of the Twentieth Century, and perhaps the greatest of any century.[23]

Bultmann's fame—some would say notoriety—was probably due to his association with the mythical view of the gospel.[24] Fully aware of the fate of David F. Strauss, who in the nineteenth century advocated the mythical view of the gospels thereby ending his teaching career,[25] Bultmann bravely espoused the mythical nature

---

22. Norman Perrin, *The New Testament: An Introduction*, (New York, Chicago, San Francisco, Atlanta: Harcourt Brace Javanovich, Inc., 1974), pp. 19, 20.

23. Norman Perrin, *The Promise of Bultmann*, (Philadelphia: Fortress Press, 1969), p. 4.

24. Kerygma and Myth, *A Theological Debate* by Rudolf Bultmann, and Ernst Lohmeyer, Julius Schniewind, Helmut Thielicke and Austin Farrer, Edited by Hans Werner Bartsch, Revised edition of this translation by Reginald H. Fuller (New York: Harper Torch books/The Cloister Library, Harper and Brothers, 1961), pp. 1-44.

25. David Friedrich Strauss, *The Life of Jesus Critically Examined*, Translated from the Fourth German edition by George Eliot, edited by Peter C. Hodgson, Philadelphia: Fortress Press, 1972), passim.

INTRODUCTION

of the gospels and their ultimate origin in the missionary preaching of the early followers of Jesus. In his program of demythologizing the gospels and the New Testament writings as a whole, Bultmann utilized existentialist philosophy in an effort to make these ancient books relevant to modern man, which propelled him to the center of Protestant Critical Theology.[26]

Bultmann developed his proclamation (preaching) theology under the banner of the Kerygma, a Greek word meaning, "proclamation" or preaching.[27] Martin Dibelius, the co-originator of the Form Critical method of the Gospel Studies, even entitled one chapter of his book, *Sermons*.[28] The verbal form of the term Kerygma (preaching) is used a total of 14 times[29] in Mark, about half as much as the word for teaching. One of Bultmann's followers, Roy A. Harrisville, even claimed that Mark is a sermon, and applied Bultmann's theories about early "Christianity" to the Gospel of Mark in an effort to clarify its meaning.[30] However, he dealt only with the content of the gospel and did not discuss the rhetorical forms Mark used to express that content.

Bultmann claimed that Jesus preached the Kingdom of God and his followers preached salvation through Jesus. Then he reduced this notion to a catchy slogan, "The proclaimer became the proclaimed."[31] Although Bultmann's followers claimed that the

26. Norman Perrin, *The Promise of Bultmann*, pp. 1–98. A concise but excellent presentation of Bultmann Theology.

27. Norman Perrin, *The New Testament An Introduction*, p. 19, note 6.; Preaching, not proclamation, is a better translation of the Greek word kerygma. Proclamation has more of a connotation of a single authoritative announcement such as Lincoln's Emancipation Proclamation. We would rarely, if ever call a preacher's sermon a proclamation.

28. Martin Dibelius, *From Tradition to Gospel*, translated from the Revised Second German Edition by Bertram Lee Woolf, (New York: Charles Scribner's Sons), pp. 9–36.

29. Vincent Taylor, *The Gospel According to St. Mark*, (Macmillan, St. Martin's Press, 1972), p. 681. The noun form of the word, kerygma, does not occur in Mark at all.

30. Roy A. Harrisville, *The Miracle of Mark*, pp. 15–23. This book is a literary not a rhetorical approach to Mark.

31. Norman Perrin, *The Promise of Bultmann*, p. 55.

gospels originated in missionary preaching designed to convert Jews and Gentiles, they did not look for the argumentative forms, the use of which was highly recommended if not obligatory, for any persuasive speech written in the Greek language.[32]

Several of Bultmann's followers went so far as to deny the presence of rational arguments in Mark's preaching. They claimed that Mark indulged in authoritative proclamation instead of reasonable argumentation to convince his opponents. According to Perrin,

> When we encounter the words of Jesus in history, we do not judge them by a philosophical system with reference to their rational validity; they meet us with the question of how we are to interpret our own experience.[33]

Roy Harrisville announced emphatically,

> For the scribe, precedent was needed to nail down the argument. When Jesus mounted the pulpit, he spoke out without marshaling the evidence of hoary antiquity to support him.[34]

George A. Kennedy in his book, *New Testament Interpretation through Rhetorical Criticism* wrote,

> The Gospel of Mark is an example of what may be called radical Christian rhetoric, a form of "sacred language" characterized by assertion and absolute claims of authoritative truth without evidence or logical argument.[35]

The case of James Robinson is more complicated and I will discuss it in detail in Chapter V, which deals with Complex rhetorical arguments.

---

32. James M. Robinson, *The Problem of History in Mark and Other Marcan Studies*, (Philadelphia: Fortress Press, 1982), p. 98.

33. Norman Perrin, *The Promise of Bultmann*, p. 98.

34. Roy A. Harrisville, *The Miracle of Mark*, pp. 40, 41.

35. George A. Kennedy, *New Testament Interpretation through Rhetorical Criticism*, (Chapel Hill and London: The University of North Carolina Press, 1984), p. 104.

INTRODUCTION

Finally, there is another reason why George A. Kennedy failed to see these argumentative forms in Mark. It must be remembered that Kennedy's work is a cross-disciplinary study and a very good one at that. However, like any such interdisciplinary research—including my own—Kennedy confronted a particular hazard that accompanies any such task. While he was very creative in rhetoric, his chosen field, when he entered New Testament Studies, he accepted the most prominent theology of the day, which happened to be Bultmann's, more or less uncritically. In spite of this handicap it is remarkable how often he was able to apply rhetorical concepts to the New Testament.

Any comprehensive view of Mark should explain why the gospel has no birth story of Jesus, which I will do in Chapter I. In Chapter II, I will translate the first word of Mark as "(a or the) guiding principle" instead of "(The) beginning," and explain why the mistranslation was overlooked for so long. In Chapter III, I will show what difference it makes; in Chapter IV, I will demonstrate Mark's use of the Greek rhetorical forms of argumentation; in Chapter V, I will discuss Mary Ann Tolbert's view of complex enthymemes or rhetorical arguments in Mark; in Chapter VI, I identify the syllogism that generated the parabolic structure of Mark, resulting in a twice-told tale; in Chapter VII, I clarify the role of Elijah in Mark's gospel; in Chapter VIII, I explain the role of John "the Baptist" in the Gospel of John, and finally Appendix II of my first book will serve as the conclusion to this one.

However, before I consider what Mark's gospel contains, I will explain what the gospel does not have, namely, a birth story of Jesus.

Chapter I

The Beginning

Why Mark Has No Birth Story of Jesus

IN JESUS' DAY THERE were at least three ways one could become a son of God: by having a lineage that led back to God (Lk. 3:38), by having God as one's immediate father (Matt 1:18, Lk 1:35), or by being rewarded at death for a lifetime of achievement (like Roman Emperors, philosophers, and heroes; Mk 15:39).

Like the Gospel of John, but unlike Matthew and Luke, Mark has no birth story of Jesus. If we had only the gospels of Mark and John, we would have no Christmas, no nativity, and no genealogy of Jesus showing that he was descended from King David.

So how did Mark explain how and when Jesus became the Son of God? In this regard, two passages are especially relevant: the one in which Jesus rejected his natural family in favor of his true family, the ones who did the will of God (Mk 3:35), and the one in which Jesus argued that the Messiah could not have been the son of David because David called him his Lord (Mk 12:35–37).

Resurrection as Translation

If Mark had Jesus become the Son of God by some process other than birth, there would have been no birth story to tell. It so happens that Mark did explain how Jesus' followers became his brothers, sisters, and mothers and it was not by a birth (or even a re-birth) process. Jesus' family heard about his activities and that people thought that he was insane so they came to take him home. When Jesus was told that his family was outside the house where he was staying, he did not invite them in, but instead asked, "Who are my mother and my brothers?" (Mk 3:33). Then he answered his own question by pointing to the ones seated around him and saying, "Whoever does the will of God is my brother and sister and mother" (Mk 3:35). The father was not mentioned presumably because God would be their father.

If Jesus' followers became a part of the family of God by doing the will of God, then Jesus probably became the Son of God in the same manner by doing the will of God by dying on the cross. In the garden of Gethsemane, Jesus prayed to God to let him live, but added, ". . .not what I will but what you will" (Mk 14:36). In other words, Jesus was not born the Son of God, but achieved that status by doing the will of God by dying on the cross, which, of course, ruled out a birth story for the Son of God at least.

Surprisingly, all this would imply that Mark did not consider Jesus the Son of God during his lifetime, but only at his death. It was when the centurion at the cross saw how Jesus died that he said, "Truly, this man was God's son" (Mk 15:39). This view would also explain the scarcity of the title Son of God in Mark. If Jesus achieved this status by his death on the cross, it could only be hinted at during his lifetime by demons blurting it out (Mk 3:11) and by God's declaring it as his baptism, Jesus' symbolic death (Mk 1:11), and at his transfiguration, his symbolic resurrection/parousia (Mk 9:7).

This view also agrees with the early Christology in Paul's letters and acts in which Jesus' exaltation to divine status was placed at his death and resurrection and not at his birth. In his letter to the Romans, Paul wrote:

> . . .descended from David according to the flesh and was declared to be the Son of God with power according to the spirit of holiness by resurrection from the dead . . . (Rom 1:3–4).

Scholars agree that Paul is here quoting an early "Christian" creed that claimed that Jesus was designated or appointed the Son of God at his resurrection. The RSV has chosen to translate the key word declared to be the Son of God, the assumption being that Jesus was already the Son of God during his lifetime and was only declared to be such at his resurrection. To translate the word in question as designated or appointed implies that Jesus was not the Son of God during his lifetime, but was designated such at his resurrection. Although Paul spoke of Jesus' pre-existence elsewhere, he did not describe him as the Son of God during his lifetime; instead, he referred to Jesus as being in "the form of a slave," "in human form," and "according to the flesh" (Phil. 2:7; 2 Cor. 5:16). Peter, speaking on the Day of Pentecost, said, "Therefore, let the entire house of Israel know with certainty that God has made him both Lord and Messiah, this Jesus whom you crucified" (Acts 2:36).

After discussing this early Christology in Paul's Letters and Acts, Raymond Brown noted that even in Mark, it was only after Jesus' death that he was finally clearly revealed to be the Son of God. Then he added, "Thus Mark has partially preserved the older understanding."[1] But why only partially? Why not completely? It would appear that Brown failed to develop the implications of this insight in relation to the Gospel of Mark. In her massive study of resurrection in the New Testament, Pheme Perkins also treated at some length the concept of resurrection as translation. Perkins claimed that when Luke describes Jesus' resurrection as translation he "has taken a Christian datum and made it intelligible to his audience by using a widely available literary model."[2] This distinction between Luke's "Christian datum" and the "literary model" held by his audience is illegitimate. Why not simply assume that Luke shared the views of his audience?

---

1. Raymond Brown, *The Birth of the Messiah* (New Haven and London: The Anchor Yale Bible, Yale University Press, 1993), pp. 29–31. See also Martin Hengel, *The Son of God*, (Philadelphia: Fortress Press, 1976), p. 59f.

2. Pheme Perkins, *Resurrection, New Testament Witness and Contemporary Reflection*, (New York: Doubleday and Company, Inc. Garden City NY, 1984), pp. 150 and 186 n.4.

The Beginning

According to Adela Yarbro Collins, what we are dealing with here is a broad cultural phenomenon. Like the Greco-Roman heroes, philosophers, and emperors, Jesus acquired his divine status by translation to heaven from the grave. Collins's own statement of the matter cannot be improved upon

> Rather, the narrative pattern according to which Jesus died, was buried, and then was translated to heaven was a culturally defined way for an author living in the first century to narrate the resurrection of Jesus.[3]

On the same page, she also wrote:

> If according to Mark, Jesus was translated from the grave to heaven, then there was no period of time during which the risen Jesus walked the earth and met with his disciples.[4]

For Mark, resurrection was an eschatological event that coincided with the end of the world. When the Son of Man appeared, it would be from heaven; he contemplated no post-resurrection appearance of Jesus except at his coming as the Son of Man.

David's Son or God's Son?

A second reason why Mark did not have a birth story of Jesus may seem even more indirect, but since it is consistent with the view expressed here, it is worth noting. Mark had Jesus argue that since David called the Messiah his Lord, he could not be his son because a father does not address his son with a superior title. The passage reads as follows:

> While Jesus was teaching in the Temple, he said "How can the scribes say that the Messiah is the son of David? David himself, by the Holy Spirit declared: "The Lord

---

3. Adela Yarbro Collins, *The Beginning of the Gospel, Probings of Mark in Context*, (Minneapolis: Fortress Press, 1992), p. 147. See also the "Excursus: Resurrection in Ancient Cultural Contexts" in her *Mark: A Commentary*, (Augsburg: Fortress Press, 2007), pp. 782–794.

4. Yarbro Collins, *The Beginning of the Gospel*, p. 147.

(God) said to my Lord (the Messiah), Sit at my right hand, until I put Your enemies under your feet. David himself calls him Lord; so how can he be his son?" and the large crowd was listening to him with delight (Mk 12:35–37, RSV).

Of course, there are assumptions here that we may not accept such as that David wrote the Psalm on which Mark's Jesus based his argument (Ps. 110:1), or the culturally conditioned belief that a father cannot address his son with an exalted title. However, if we entertain these notions in order to understand Mark's logic, the Messiah could not be the son of anyone else who called him Lord. The same reasoning would apply to all of the early followers of Jesus who came to call him Lord. Of course, if Jesus were not the son of David, there would be no need for a genealogy showing he was, and if he became the Son of God through his achievements, there would be no need for a birth story showing his divine origin.

Jesus' Genealogy and Birth Story in Matthew

Finally, we need to ask how Matthew can have a birth story and genealogy. In other words, just what did Matthew find inadequate in Mark's view? Without a birth story, Mark's designation of Jesus as the Son of God could easily have been "confused" with the "honorific" use of the title among the Greeks and Romans. As we have already seen, in that view, one did not usually become the Son of God by birth, but achieved that status by one's life activities, and it was conferred on one at death. By the birth story of Jesus, Matthew made clear that Jesus was the Son of God at his birth and during his lifetime. The apparent divine absence in Mark, in power at least (Mk 9:1), was intolerable to Matthew so he also called Jesus Emmanuel, or, God with Us (Matt 1:23).[5]

The views of both Mark and Matthew are intelligible when we take into account the conditions under which each wrote. In my opinion, Matthew belonged to Mark's community, and even

---

5. Mark Allen Powell, *God with Us: A Pastoral Theology of Matthew's Gospel*, (Minneapolis: Fortress Press, 1995), passim.

succeeded him as a teacher there. Scholars believe that Matthew wrote in Syria, if not in Antioch itself. One of the considerations pointing in that direction is that Ignatius of Antioch quoted a few passages from Matthew. This view is clearly expressed in Thomas G. Long's book on Matthew.

> However, the most frequent suggestion is that Matthew's church was located in Antioch of Syria, a sizeable metropolis with a large, mixed population. The fact that Ignatius, the Bishop of Antioch, seems to know the Gospel of Matthew and to quote from it as early as AD 110 favors this view.[6]

Since Matthew incorporated almost the entire Gospel of Mark in his own gospel, and even issued a revised edition of that Gospel , it is probable that Matthew belonged to Mark's community in Syria.

The differences between the two gospels can easily be accounted for by the fact that Mark wrote slightly before, during, or shortly after the war between Rome and Judea circa 60CE, and Matthew wrote some times after that event. Even if Mark wrote at the time of the war, his views, no doubt, were formed and matured prior to the war when the temple state still existed and a wider spectrum of opinion was tolerated. Writing sometime after the war, Matthew participated along with formative Judaism in a conservative reaction against Greco-Roman culture, the enemy's culture.[7] Something analogous happened in American public opinion after 9/11 with Islamic religion replacing Greco-Roman culture. Matthew shared the Pharisee's belief in the Davidic descent of the Messiah, so when he turned away from Mark's "Hellenistic" view of how Jesus became the Son of God, he also "rejected" Mark's argument against the Davidic descent of the Messiah, if he even noticed it. Instead, Matthew combined a genealogy in which Jesus descended from David through Joseph with a birth story in

---

6. Thomas G. Long, *Matthew*, (Louisville and London: Westminster John Knox Press, 1997), p. 3.

7. J. Andrew Overman, *Matthew's Gospel and Formative Judaism: The Social World of the Matthean Community*, (Augsburg Fortress Press, 1990), passim.

which Jesus was conceived directly by God's Spirit thereby becoming the Son of God.

The frequently repeated claim that Matthew is the most Jewish gospel is only valid if we are careful to specify the Judaism about which we are speaking. While Matthew resembled the post-war Judaism of the Pharisees or Rabbinic Judaism, Mark reflected the pre-war Judaism in which the Pharisees competed with a number of other sects such as the Sadducees, Essenes, Zealots, and the followers of Jesus. In this situation in which there were a number of choices, Mark could not simply assert his beliefs; he found it necessary to make an extended argument for them. We will now consider the beginning of Mark's argument.

Chapter II

Arché

Why the First Word of Mark was Mistranslated as "Beginning"

Beginning or Guiding Principle?

ALTHOUGH NONE OF THE other three canonical gospels, Matthew, Luke, or John quoted the first verse of Mark, all three appear to have been aware of its first word, arché, "beginning," and reflected it in their own gospels in various ways. Too often the diverse ways the four gospels introduced Jesus' story are presented as curiosities with no further implications to be drawn from it. Usually scholars called attention to *when* each gospel author began the story of Jesus: Mark with John the Baptist, Matthew with Jesus' ancestry and birth, Luke with John the Baptist's birth, and finally John with Jesus' pre-existence in the beginning with God. J. Ramsey Michaels put it this way:

> Each of the four Gospels begins appropriately enough, with a reference to some kind of beginning. Mark's heading is "Beginning of the gospel of Jesus Christ" (Mk. 1:1). Matthew opens with "an account of the origin of Jesus Christ" (Mt. 1:1). Luke acknowledges the traditions of "those who from the beginning were eyewitnesses and ministers of the word" (Lk 1:2). John's "beginning" (arché)

is *the earliest of all*, for the vocabulary of John's preamble is decisively shaped by the opening verses of Genesis.[1]

Matthew appears to have objected to Mark's beginning Jesus' story with John the Baptist instead of Jesus. Therefore, Matthew began with a genealogy of Jesus and proceeded with the demotion of the Baptist that in John's gospel reached astonishing proportions. When Jesus came to be baptized by John the Baptist, Matthew wrote:

> John would have prevented him, saying, "I need to be baptized by you, and do you come to me?" But Jesus answered him, "Let it be so now; for it is proper for us in this way to fulfill all righteousness." Then he consented. (Matt. 3:13–15).

After John was incarcerated, Jesus praised the Baptist, calling him "more than a prophet" (Matt. 11:9), and even Elijah, saying: "Truly I tell you, among those born of women, no one has arisen greater than John the Baptist" (Matt. 11:11a). . ."and if you are willing to accept it, he is Elijah who is to come" (Matt. 11:14).Then Matthew had Jesus qualify this high praise of the Baptist by adding, "yet the least in the Kingdom of Heaven is greater than he" (Matt. 11:11b).

Instead of beginning his gospel with John the Baptist, Matthew began his story of Jesus with a genealogy reaching back to King David and beyond to Abraham and the story of Jesus' birth. Matthew may even have changed Mark's first word, arché to birth (Matt. 1:18), and origin or ancestry (Matt. 1:1). Whereas Mark had Jesus become the Son of God at his death, Matthew had Jesus become "God with us" through his birth (Matt. 1:23).

While Mark described Jesus as the absent bridegroom (Mk. 2:20), Matthew comforted his community with the words: "For where two or three are gathered together in my name, I am there among you" (Matt. 18:20).

---

1. J. Ramsey Michaels, *The Gospel of John, The New International Commentary on the New Testament* (Grand Rapids, Michigan/Cambridge, UK: William B. Eerdmans Publishing Company, 2010), p. 46. See also James McGowan, *The Gospel of Mark, Christ the Servant*, (Chattanooga, TN: Published by AMG Publishers, 2006), p. 46.

Finally, Matthew found Mark's empty tomb and absent Lord (Mk. 16:6), intolerable and consoled his community with Jesus' promise: "and remember I am with you always, to the end of the age" (Matt. 28:20b).

In contrast, Mark had the young man at the empty tomb say, "He is not here" (Mk. 16:6). This continuing presence of Jesus as "God with us" prevented Matthew from sensing the temporal distance between the time of Jesus and his own day. Matthew said that the chief priests explained Jesus resurrection by creating a rumor that Jesus' disciples stole his body, "and this story is still told among the Jews *to this day*" (Matt. 28:15b). This is the closest Matthew came to acknowledging any passage of time since Jesus' day.

Although Mark, Matthew, and John's gospels reflected some awareness of the period since Jesus' day, it was with Luke that this epoch became a guiding principle in the composition of a gospel. If Mark's "arché," "beginning," introduced the gospel of Jesus Christ, Luke's "ap'archés," "from the beginning," introduced the period of the gathering together, organizing, and writing down of the tradition. Because Luke wrote at some temporal distance from the events themselves, he felt the need to appeal to the numerous accounts that were handed down "ap'archés," "from (the) beginning" by the eyewitnesses and servants of the word. By "investigating everything carefully, from the very first," or from the beginning, Luke hoped to persuade Theophilus that the teaching that he had received was true.

Matthew carried the genealogy of Jesus back to Abraham, but John's gospel had Jesus say, "Before Abraham was, I am" (Jn. 8:58). Mark put John the Baptist in "(the) beginning of the gospel" (Mk. 1:1), but John's gospel placed the Logos (the Word) in the beginning with God (Jn. 1:1). The author of the Fourth gospel objected to Mark's making John the Baptist the beginning of the gospel instead of Jesus, which explains the Fourth gospel's exaltation of Jesus and demotion of John the Baptist. While Matthew carried Jesus' genealogy back to Abraham, Luke ended his genealogy of Jesus with the "son of Adam, son of God" (Lk. 3:38). Since I will deal with the Fourth gospel's reaction to Mark's gospel at some length, I will defer its treatment until the discussion of Mark's view is complete. In my opinion, it is very possible, if not probable, that Matthew's "origin," Luke's from the beginning, and John's "In the beginning" stem from Mark's first word, (the) beginning.

If Mark did not begin his gospel with a genealogy or birth story, just how did he begin it? Scholars noticed that Mark's story of Jesus began with John the Baptist, so they thought the first word of Mark, arché, referred to the ministry of the Baptist, and translated it as "the" beginning," to provide the story with a chronological starting point. However, as I will soon demonstrate, the quotation formula, "as it is written" links the first word of Mark not with John the Baptist, but with the "Isaiah" prophecy and should be translated "guiding principle" in order to provide the gospel with a logical starting point. This would imply that Mark is an argumentative discourse rather than a biography, novel, or drama.

Although a few scholars have discussed the alternate meanings of arché as guiding or first principle, most if not all of the standard English translations/revisions of Mark since the 16th Century mistranslated arché as beginning, and incorrectly constructed and incorrectly punctuated the first paragraph of Mark's gospel. This translation persisted despite the current lack of consensus about the meaning of arché translated as beginning. It is unclear whether "the beginning" referred to John the Baptist's ministry alone or also included those of Jesus, Paul, and the early church. C.H. Turner claimed that, "in general, modern exegetes are more or less agreed in segregating verse 1 as a sort of title, though it is hard to see what real meaning arché has on this supposition."[2]

One reason scholars claimed that the first line of Mark is a title is that the first word omitted the article and Verse 1 has no verb. However, Greek has no indefinite article and simply omits the definite article when the indefinite article is intended. Of course, this would not make much sense with the translation "(a) beginning of the gospel," but makes perfect sense with the translation "(a) guiding principle," but the choice of which article was

---

2. C. H. Turner, "Marcan Usage: Notes, Critical and Exegetical, on the Second Gospel," *J.T.L. XXVI* (19250, p. 146.

intended is still in doubt because Greek sometimes also omits the definite article with the understanding that the reader will supply it. Three other times Mark used the word arché without the article and the RSV supplied it in each case (Mk 10:6, 13:8, 13:19). When the main verb is the verb "to be," and is omitted, sometimes the reader is expected to supply it as well.[3]

Allen Wikgren, one of the editors of the Nestle/Aland Greek New Testament, suggested that the alternate logical meaning of arché might provide a better translation. The root meaning of arché appears to have been priority, which gave rise to three derivative meanings: personal priority being "ruler or ruling authority," chronological priority "beginning," and logical priority, "guiding principle."

In his book on Aristotle, John Herman Randall, Jr. had this to say about the meaning of arché in Greek: When Aristotle set about to make an argument regarding various matters, he demonstrated,

> . . .them from things that come before the conclusions, and are hence logically prior to those conclusions. . . . arché in Greek means "beginning." As Aristotle says, a quarrel is the "beginning" of a fight; and a keel is the "beginning" or arché of a ship. Arché meant also "rule" or "control;" and this connotation also enters into the flavor of Aristotle's "beginnings" of demonstration. These archai of demonstration and science appeared in Latin as "principia" or principles—the Latin term for "beginnings." In English, they mean the "beginnings" of understanding and intelligibility.[4]

Randall is obviously using the word "beginning" in the logical, not the chronological, sense. The Oxford Dictionary defines a principle as "a fundamental truth or law as the basis of reasoning or action (arguing from first principles. . .)." Modern scientists arrive at

---

3. Nigel Turner, *Grammatical Insights into the New Testament*, (London New York: T&T Clark International, 1965, reprint, 1994, this ed. 2004), p.28. See also Elizabeth Struthers Malbon, *Hearing Mark: A Listener's Guide* (Harrisburg, Penn.: Trinity Press International, 2002), p.11.

4. John Herman Randall, Jr., *Aristotle*, (New York: Columbia University Press, 1960), p. 35.

such rules or principles through inductive studies guided by hypotheses. Then they use deductive reasoning to develop theories such as evolution. In contrast, ancient philosophers slighted inductive observation and drew their first principles from tradition combined with a few obvious observations. Since they did not systematically submit these principles to empirical tests, they frequently accepted false notions as true, such as Aristotle's mistaken belief about falling bodies. The author of the Gospel of Mark accepted just such a traditional principle drawn from the Old Testament and contained in the Messenger prophecy (Mk. 1:2–3).

Probable arguments and absolute conclusions

If, as I believe, Mark intended to establish his case to a certainty, how could he do that with rhetorical arguments that produced only probable and not absolute conclusions? The difficulty in achieving certainty had to do with the problem of premises. How could one be sure that they were true? Aristotle had suggested that one's guiding principles be taken from the opinions of great men in the past. As John Herman Randall, Jr. put it, "The archai to be examined are the "accepted opinions," the endoxa, "of the most notable and illustrious men."[5] The authority of these eminent thinkers of the past insured the acceptance of their opinions, which could then be used as premises in arguments. However, because of the complexity and ambiguity of political, legal, and religious issues, one could ordinarily reach only probable conclusions in these areas. If one could establish one's case absolutely, there would be no room for argument, because argumentation occurs in areas in which absolute certainty is not attainable. Therefore, unlike Aristotle, who based his reasoning on human opinions, Mark based his argument on divine authority. As his guiding principle, he chose a passage from Isaiah:

> A voice cries out:
> "In the wilderness prepare the way of the Lord,
> Make straight in the desert a highway for our God (Is. 40:3)

---

5. *Ibid.*, p. 44.

If Mark had founded his argument on this passage alone, he would not have based it on divine authority, because the voice that cried out was human. When Mark added Exodus 23:20 to the Isaiah prophecy, he made the speaker of the prophecy God himself, instead of "the voice," which was now placed in the wilderness and identified as the messenger, who prepared the way of the Lord.

> *Behold, I send an angel* [messenger] *before you* to guard you on the way (Exo. 23:20).

Mark is no longer basing his argument on the word of a prophet, but on a divine declaration. By having the messenger go before the Lord, Mark established the order of their appearance as the guiding principle of his argument for Jesus' Messiahship.

Finally, by adding the passage from Malachi, Mark implicitly identified the Messenger as Elijah. "Behold, I will send my messenger and he will prepare the way before me" (Mal. 3:1); "Behold, I will send Elijah the prophet before the great and awesome day of the Lord comes" (Mal. 4:5).

By placing the story of John the Baptist and Jesus immediately after the prophecy, Mark identified John and Jesus as the messenger and the Lord. Since Mark based his argument on a promise of God himself, it is doubtful that he considered his conclusions merely probable. What's more important, Mark's audience probably shared his view of scripture and accepted his conclusions as well.

Why the Logical Meaning of Arché Was Overlooked

Before we proceed with a consideration of the further implications of this view, it is necessary to deal with a rather obvious objection that might be raised against it. After all, the chronological translation of arché as "beginning" has stood for hundreds of years. If the translation of the first word of Mark as "guiding principle" makes so much sense, why was it overlooked for so long? My first task will be to explain just that, which I propose to do by answering the following three questions: Why was arché translated as "beginning" in the first place; why did translators (the experts) not consider the logical meaning of the word, and did anyone get it right?

Why was arché translated as "beginning" in the first place?

When the early translators rendered the first word of Mark as "beginning," they apparently took it to indicate the chronological starting point of the gospel story of Jesus. The translation persisted because Mark was usually considered some kind of story (history, biography, or fiction), and a story needed a chronological beginning. When the Enlightenment thinkers of the "Age of Reason" created a non-miraculous "history" of Jesus, they gave reasons for accepting or rejecting various parts of the story. However, as a narrative it still needed a chronological starting point, so there was no reason to question the translation of arché as "beginning." Finally, literary critics came to treat Mark as fiction (a novel or drama), which also cannot dispense with a temporal beginning. Scholars were apparently led astray by their focus on Mark's story of Jesus to the neglect of his encompassing persuasive argumentative discourse, which required a logical guiding principle.

Why Did Translators (The Experts) Not Consider the Logical Meaning of Arché?

Of course, translators were also influenced by the prevailing conception of Mark as story, but why did their philological or linguistic training not kick in? After all, they were translating from the Greek manuscripts, were they not? Not necessarily! Actually, many "translations" are not translations at all, but rather revisions of earlier versions or translations, from the King James Version to the Revised Standard Version. Bruce Metzger, a prominent textual scholar, pointed out:

> 80 percent or more of the English Bible down through the Revised Version has been estimated to be...Tyndale's

sixteenth century translation in. . .those portions of the Bible on which he had work with such skill and devotion.[6]

The current translation of arché as beginning appears to stem from Wycliffe's 14th Century translation from Latin, the bigynnynge, and Tyndale's 16th Century translation from Greek, "the beginnynge." Meanwhile, the spelling of "beginning" has been standardized.[7]

Even individual translations or versions of Mark did not vary significantly from this pattern set in the 14th and 16th centuries. Of the 35 versions of Mark surveyed by Pearl Sjo[set umlaut over o]landers, 22 have "(The) beginning," 4 "beginning," 1 "The First Word," 2 "begins," 3 "Here begins," 1 "started," 1 "It began," and 1 omitted the first line of Mark altogether.[8]

Therefore, in the standard translations/versions of the Bible, and in many if not most, of the individual "translations," the rendering of arché as "(The) beginning," remained the same from the 14th Century to the present.

The reasons for this are simple. The revisers had two main concerns: to base the text on older, more reliable manuscripts, and update words whose meaning had changed or become archaic or obsolete. An example of the former, the better manuscripts, Sinaiticus and Vaticanus did not contain Mark 16:9–20, so the passage was no longer considered a part of Mark's gospel. Examples of the latter are the words "gospel," which is now translated "good news," and "Holy Ghost," which is now translated "Holy Spirit." However, the word "beginning" had not changed in meaning since the 14th Century, but was simply the wrong word in the first place.

Another circumstance that could have diverted reviser's attention is that the two applicable meanings of arché are represented

---

6. Bruce M. Metzger, *The Bible in Translation Ancient and English Versions*, (Grand Rapids, Michigan: Baker Academic, A Division of Baker Book House Co., 2001), p. 60.

7. Ibid., pp. 56–58.

8. Pearl Sjo[set umlaut over o]lander, *Some Aspects of Style in Twentieth-Century English Bible Translation One-Man Versions of Mark and the Psalms*, (Umia, 1979), pp. 181–95.

in English by two different words: "beginning" and "first principle" or "guiding principle." If the Greek word had been used for the logical meaning of arché instead of the Latin derived word "principle," we would now speak about the archai of biology or physics instead of the principles of biology or physics, and we would call William James' classical work "The Archai of Psychology" rather than "The Principles of Psychology." The Greek word arché was not used for either meaning in English, but does appear in such words as "archaeology," "archaic," and "archaeopteryx."

Did Anyone Get it Right?

If no one else got it right, it might be problematic; I might even be compelled to reconsider my view. However, a minority has noticed that arché has other meanings than beginning. While only a few have adopted an alternate translation of arché, what they lack in numbers they make up in importance: James A. Kleist, a professor of classical languages, translated arché as "a summary."[9] Allen Wikgren, one of the editors of the Nestle/Aland Greek New Testament referred to Kleist approvingly and translated arché as "first thing" in the sense of "rudiments" or "elements" or "essentials" of the gospel.[10]

Michael Patella, Associate Professor of New Testament at St. John's University rendered arché as "origin, first cause, earthly, or spiritual reigning power or authority, rule or elementary principle."[11] Next, Mary Ann Beavis in her commentary recognized that the first word of Mark has a diversity of meanings:

> The word arché that abruptly announces the beginning of Mark has a range of meanings that include "first causes," "ruler," and "rule" in the abstract sense of office

---

9. James A. Kleist, *The Memoirs of St. Peter of the Gospel According to St. Mark, Translated into English Sense-Lines*, (Milwaukee, NY, Chicago: The Bruce Publishing Co., 1931), p. 65.

10. Allen Wikgren, "ΑΡΧΗ ΤΟΥ ΕΥΑΓΓΕΛΙΟΥ," p. 7.

11. Michael Patella, *Mithras, Paul and the Gospel of Mark*, (New York and London: T&T Clark, 2006), p. 32.

ARCHÉ

or function: If 1:1 is a title for the whole document, then the whole document ought to be considered the arché (Boring 1990, 53).[12]

Others combined two of the three available choices: Mark Horne, a minister, had "beginning and first principle,"[13] and Daniel J. Harrington and John R. Donahue in their massive commentary on Mark opted for "beginning and rule."[14] Finally, Joel Marcus was the one who came closest to a correct translation of Mark's introduction. Marcus claimed:

> One of *the organizing principles* of this Markan Composition seems to be the demonstration that *the beginning* of the good news *happened* "as it has been written in Isaiah the prophet" (Mk 1:2).[15]

By using both "organizing principle" and "beginning" he has simply translated arché twice. He could have dispensed with "beginning," in which case the organizing principle did not "happen" in accordance with the prophecy (Mk. 1:2–3), but was the prophecy. The verb "to be" and not an action verb was called for. Although a few scholars translated arché as "first principle," none, to my knowledge, drew the inferences for the interpretation of Mark. Nor did this translation make it into the standard versions of the Bible.[16]

Before we continue, we must ask what difference one word can make. In a treaty, it can make the difference between war and

12. Mary Ann Beavis, *Mark*, (Grand Rapids, Michigan: Baker Academic, 2011), p. 40.

13. Mark Horne, *The Victory According to Mark*, (Moscow, ID: Canon Press, 2003), p. 43.

14. Daniel J. Harrington and John R. Donahue, S.J., *The Gospel of Mark, Sacra Pagina Series, V. 2* (Collegeville, Minnesota: A Michael Glazier Book, The Liturgical Press, 2002), pp. 59–60.

15. Joel Marcus, *Mark 1–8: A New Translation with Introduction and Commentary by Joel Marcus, The Anchor Bible, Vol. 27* (New York: Doubleday, 2000), p. 139.

16. See C.E.B. Cranfield, *The Gospel According to St. Mark*, (London: Cambridge University Press, 1959), p. 34, for ten different solutions to the problem of arché, and Mark 1:1.

peace. In a pre-nuptial agreement it can also mean the difference between war and peace and poverty and riches. We will now attempt to explain what difference it makes in the understanding of the Gospel of Mark.

Chapter III

What difference does it make?

How much difference one wrong word can make depends on where it occurs. In an introduction, in which an author is presumably stating his theme or purpose explicitly, it is calculated to do maximum damage. Unless the introduction is clear, it may not be possible to determine the author's intention as he develops it implicitly throughout the body of the work. The reverse side of this is that the correct translation of arché as guiding principle can be expected to have an enormous impact on the interpretation not only of Mark's introduction, but also of the entire gospel. As for Mark's introduction, the new translation affects its punctuation and syntax, its form, its length, and its clarity. The impact on the body of the gospel is equally great suggesting that we have to do with a persuasive speech, which employed Greek rhetorical forms of argumentation. It will be found that an enthymeme or rhetorical syllogism generated the parabolic structure of Mark's persuasive speech with the result that the story of John the Baptist and Jesus was told twice. The new translation of arché also clarifies the role of Elijah in Mark and the role of John "the Baptist" in the Gospel of John.

Nestle Versus Tischendorf: A Question of Punctuation

The biggest obstacle to understanding Mark's introduction is the widely held notion that the first line of Mark is a title, since the first word has no article and the verse has no verb. The line reads, "(The) beginning of the gospel of Jesus Christ (Son of God)."*(Mk, 1:1)* One of the more interesting interpretations of this verse is that of Elizabeth Malbon Struthers. She compared it to the announcement of "The President of the United States"[1] However, there is no parallel here as Mark did not write, "The Gospel of Jesus Christ," but "The *beginning* of the gospel of Jesus Christ." Struthers omitted the first word of Mark, which if translated as "beginning" qualifies the gospel temporally, and if translated as "guiding principle," qualifies the gospel logically. Two pages later, Struthers discussed the first word of Mark, but her discussion did not affect her understanding of the verse.[2]

The faulty punctuation of the RSV stems from its use of the Nestle-Aland Greek New Testament, which has been used so widely and gained such a high measure of respect because it summarized the best textual criticism of the 19th Century. Its value is derived from its use of the three greatest texts of that century—Westcott-Hort, Constantine Tischendorf, the flamboyant discoverer of Sinaiticus, and Bernard Weiss.[3] Nestle simply took the majority reading of these three texts. Weymouth, a fourth text, was used earlier. Nestle appears to have used the same majority rule to arrive at the punctuation of Mark's introduction. It must be remembered that the Greek manuscripts were not punctuated, so to punctuate a text is to interpret it. In my opinion, Nestle's punctuation and syntax of Mark's introduction is a direct result of his misunderstanding of the meaning of the first word of Mark. Therefore,

---

1. Elizabeth Struthers Malbon, *Hearing Mark a Listener's Guide*, (Harrisburg, Pennsylvania: Trinity Press International, 2002), p.11.

2. Ibid., p.13.

3. Bruce M. Metzger and Bart D. Ehrman, *The Text of the New Testament, Its Transmission, Corruption, and Restoration*, Fourth Edition, (New York & Oxford: Oxford University Press, 2005), pp. 190ff.

one should reconsider Nestle's rejection of Tischendorf's punctuation. Fortunately, Nestle had a habit of writing short comments on various topics,[4] one of which concerned this matter:

> It is quite a mistake of Tischendorf to put a comma between (ver. 1) and (ver. 2) and a full stop after (ver. 3). In this respect Westcott-Hort have shown a much better judgment in printing verse 1 as some sort of heading and separating it from the following text.[5]

In my opinion, Tischendorf's judgment was correct and Nestle's, Westcott-Hort's, and Weiss's were incorrect. Nestle arrived at his own view that Mark 1:1 is a title by eliminating arché from the text of Mark altogether. He claimed that the first verse of Mark originally read, "The Gospel of Jesus Christ." Arché, Nestle said, was at first a marginal gloss that indicated where the Gospel of Mark began in a four-gospel collection. As a marginal notation it read, "Here begins," a verb that later entered the text as a noun, "(The) beginning."[6] Few have followed Nestle in this opinion.

The Form of the Introduction: "As it is Written"

When Nestle declared that the first verse of Mark was the title of the gospel, in the same short article mentioned above, he argued that the gospel's text began with the words, "As it is written," then went on to declare that, "as" or "as it is written" is "a most natural opening of a book."[7] The examples Nestle brought forward to support this assertion do perhaps prove that a book can begin with "as" but not "as it is written" because the latter contains a quotation

---

4. Warren A. Kay, "The Life and Work of Eberhard Nestle," in *The Bible As Book: The Transmission of the Greek Text*, Ed. By Scot McKendrick and Orlaith A. O'Sullivan (London: 2003), p. 192.

5. Eberhard Nestle, "How Does the Gospel of Mark Begins," *Exposition*, Fourth Series, 1984, Vol. X, p. 459.

6. Ibid., pp. 458–459.

7. Ibid., p. 459. See also M. Eugene Boring's "Mark 1:1–15 and the Beginning of the Gospel," in *How Gospels Begin*, Semeia 52, (Society of Biblical Literature, 1991), p. 48–50 for a list of ten different punctuations of Mark 1:1–4.

formula that requires a prior statement, which the subsequent authoritative quotation supports. Anderson's Commentary on Mark makes this point very clear:

> Accordingly the presumption is and it is supported by the fact that this formula always introduces a scriptural confirmation of a preceding statement, that Mark intends to apply the scripture(s) he quotes to his opening words in 1:1, and thus to demonstrate that the gospel's "beginning" (i.e. the whole story of Jesus) is in conformity with the will of God expressed in the O.T.[8]

However, Anderson also operated with an erroneous definition of arché as the beginning of "the whole story of Jesus." Joel Marcus also took exception to Nestle's view:

> Taylor (153) and others have argued that "as it has been written" is the beginning of a second sentence independent of 1:1 citing Luke 11:30, 17:26, John 3:14, and I Cor. 2:9 as parallels. As Guelich ("beginning," 5) shows, however in its Jewish occurrences as well as in its numerous N.T. usages, the formula is transitional in function, acting as a bridge between a previously mentioned fact or event and the O.T. citation that follows and confirms it.[9]

This form is confirmed by Mark's use of this quotation formula, "as it is written" two other times in his gospel: Mark 7:6 and 9:13. The first instance exhibits the complete form: statement, quotation formula, and supporting scripture. Answering the Pharisees and scribes, Jesus,

> said to them, Isaiah prophesied rightly about you hypocrites, as it is written, "this people honor me with their lips, but their hearts are far from me, in vain, do they worship me, teaching human precepts as doctrines" (Mk. 7:6, 7).

---

8. Hugh Anderson, *The Gospel of Mark*, New Century Bible Commentary, (Grand Rapids: Wm. B. Eerdmans Pub. Co., 1976) pp. 67, 68.

9. Joel Marcus, *Mark 1–8: A New Translation with Introduction and Commentary* by Joel Marcus (New York: The Anchor Bible, Vol. 27), pp. 141–142.

What difference does it make?

The second example in Mark omitted the scriptural citation, but it was clearly implied by the quotation formula. "But I tell you that Elijah has come, and they did to him whatever they please as it is written about him" (Mk 9:13).

In my book, *Mark: A Twice-Told Tale*, I discussed this passage in some detail, arguing that the scripture implied was the messenger prophecy at the beginning of Mark (Mk 1:2–3).

Matthew's parallel to the messenger prophecy did not use the quotation formula "as it is written," but Luke's did. Luke also exhibited the full form: statement, quotation formula, and supporting scripture:

> He (John the Baptist) went into all the country around the Jordan, preaching a baptism of repentance for forgiveness of sins. As it is written in the book of the words of Isaiah the Prophet: "a voice of one calling in the desert, 'Prepare the way for the Lord, make straight paths for him'" (Lk. 3:3–4).

Therefore, Luke understood that the quotation formula referred to a prior statement.

In Paul's letter to the Romans, there are 14 examples of this quotation formula (Rom. 1:17, 2:24, 3:4, 3:10, 4:17, 8:36, 9:13, 9:33, 10:15, 11:8, 11:26, 15:3, 15:9, and 15:21). In every case, the quotation formula is preceded by a statement and followed by a confirming scriptural quotation. A few examples will make this point clear:

> For I am not ashamed of the gospel; it is the power of God for salvation to everyone who has faith, to the Jew first and also to the Greek. For in it the righteousness of God is revealed through faith for faith; as it is written, "The one who is righteous will live by faith" (Rom. 1:16–17).

> And how are they to proclaim him unless they are sent? As it is written, "How beautiful are the feet of those who bring good news! (Rom. 1:14)

> Thus I make it my ambition to proclaim the good news, not where Christ has already been named, so that I do

not build on someone else's foundation, but as it is written, "Those who have never been told of him shall see, and those who have never heard of him shall understand" (Rom. 15:20–21).

Finally, G.D. Kilpatrick supports our conclusions in regards to this form. He wrote:

> Where "as" introduces a following quotation in the New Testament it invariably follows its main clause . . . Some editors break this rule in their punctuation of Mark 1:1, but there is no need to do this."[10]

The Length of the Introduction

It might be objected that Mark 1:1–3 is too short to be an adequate introduction to the gospel story of Jesus. However, I will argue that it is perfectly appropriate as an introduction to Mark's persuasive speech. R. H. Lightfoot and James M. Robinson extended the introduction from Mark 1:8 where Westcott-Hort placed it to Mark 1:13,[11] which with a further extension to verse 15 became the current consensus.[12] Whereas Westcott-Hort had a break at verse 8, when Jesus arrived to be baptized by John, the new view placed the break at verse 13 when Jesus began his ministry in Galilee. In my opinion, John's preaching and baptizing began to fulfill the messenger prophecy (Mk 1:4), so they are not part of Mark's introduction, but the beginning of the body of the gospel.

To support his view of Mark's introduction, Lightfoot compared it to the introduction to the Gospel of John, "There is thus

---

10. G. D. Kilpatrick, "The Punctuation of John VII. 37–38." *The Journal of Theological Studies*, Vol. XI, Part 2 (Oxford: At the Clareson Press, Oct. 1960), pp. 340–341.

11. R. H. Lightfoot, *The Gospel Message of St. Mark*, (Eugene, Oregon: Wipf and Stock Publishers, 2004), p. 15, 16, Previously published by Oxford University Press, 1950. See also James M. Robinson's *The Problem of History in Mark, and Other Marcan Studies*, (Philadelphia: Fortress Press, 1982), p. 70 N. I. First Published by SCM Press, Ltd., London, 1957.

12. Dennis E. Smith, Guest Editor, "How Gospels Begin," *Semeia* 52, (Published by the Society of Biblical Literature, 1991), p. 43.

a close parallel, in spite of all their differences, between these thirteen verses of Mark and the first eighteen verses of John, which are usually regarded as the prologue to that gospel."[13] In my opinion, the extension of the introduction of the Gospel of John to verse 18 may also be problematic. Our shorter introduction to Mark brings to light an unexpected parallel between Mark and John. Jan van Der Watt compared the first five verses of the Gospel of John (Jn. 1:1–5), instead of the first 18 verses (Jn. 1:1–18), with the introduction of the first letter of John (I Jn. 1:1–4), which seems to suggest that the first five verses of John's gospel could have served as its introduction at least at one stage of its composition.[14] However, a better comparison is between the first five verses of the Gospel of John and the first three verses of the Gospel of Mark.

John	Mark
In the beginning was the word, and the word was with God, and the word was God. He was in the beginning with God. All things come into being through him, and without him not one thing came into being. What has come into being in him was life, and the life was the light of all people. The light shines in the darkness, and the darkness did not overcome it.	(The) beginning of the good news of Jesus Christ the (Son of God). As it is written in the prophet Isaiah, See I am sending my messenger ahead of you, who will prepare your way; the voice of one crying out in the wilderness: Prepare the way of the Lord, make his paths straight.
(Jn. 1:1–5)	(Mk. 1:1–3)

Table 1

The parallel is confirmed by what Mark and John's gospels recorded next. After John 1:5 the Gospel of John continued with the appearance of John "the Baptist": After Mark 1:3, the Gospel of Mark also continued with the appearance of John the Baptist.

---

13. R. H. Lightfoot, *The Gospel Message of St. Mark*, p. 18.

14. Jan van der Watt, *An Introduction to the Johannine Gospel and Letters*, (New York: T&T Clark, 2007), p. 7.

| There was a man sent from God, whose name was John (Jn. 1:6). | John the Baptist appeared in the wilderness... (Mk. 1:4) |

Table 2

At this point, it is necessary to ask how long New Testament introductions usually were. A casual glance at a few such introductions will tend to cast doubt on the long introductions proposed for Mark (Mk. 1:1–13 or 15) and John (Jn. 1:1–18). Luke's introduction is only four verses long (Lk. 1:1–4). Acts is five verses long (Acts 1:1–5), Hebrews is four verses long (Heb. 1:1–4), and I John is four verses long (I Jn. 1:1–4). In a few verses, the authors stated briefly and explicitly their theme or purpose in writing, which they then developed implicitly in the body of their work.

After I wrote the above, I came across an astonishing observation by J. Ramsey Michaels on the length of the "Preamble" to John's Gospel, which I prefer to call by the ancient rhetorical term for an introduction, a "prooemium." However, Michael's views on the Logos and light in the Gospel are nothing short of prescient and go a long way towards solving the thorny problem of the Logos in that gospel. Michael's goes on to point out that the fourth gospel's story began with the arrival of John the "Baptist" on the scene. Even though I arrived at virtually the same idea independently, after which I discovered Michael's work, he outranks me because he was first. His own words cannot be improved upon. He called Jn. 1:1–5 "Preamble: The Light." Then he continued:

> The story to be told in this Gospel begins with the words, "a man came, sent from God." John was his name (Jn. 1:6). This means that the five preceding verses must be taken as a kind of preface or preamble, in keeping with the principle stated by John himself that "the one coming after me...was before me" (v. 15; see also v. 30). This will be new to generations of readers who are accustomed to setting the first eighteen verses of the Gospel apart as "the Prologue."[15]

---

15. J. Ramsey Michaels, *The Gospel of John, The New International Commentary on the New Testament*, (Grand Rapids, Michigan/ Cambridge, U.K.: William B. Eerdmans Publishing Company, 2010), p. 45.

Michaels also noticed the parallel with Mark's gospel: "The narrative, like that of Mark's Gospel (1:4), begins with John the Baptist, or Baptizer, known here simply as 'John' (v. 6)."[16] These observations would appear also to call into question the consensus that considers the first thirteen verses of Mark as the introduction to that gospel.

Clarity of Introductions: How much obscurity was tolerated in Introductions?

Related to the question of brevity is the issue of clarity. To say that an author expresses his purpose explicitly in his introduction is to say that he stated it clearly. However, few scholars bothered to raise the question as to how clear an introduction was expected to be or how much obscurity was tolerated. A quick look at the introductions to Luke's gospel (Lk. 1:1–4), reveals that a great deal of clarity was expected in an author's initial statement of his purpose. Although we may not understand everything an author intended, we readily get the gist of what he was writing. At times, there was a fairly high degree of correlation between their introduction's explicit statement of purpose and the implicit development of their stated intent in the body of the work.

No doubt Luke was following recognized conventions[17] when he referred to the many who had written accounts of Jesus' activities before him, appealed to eyewitnesses, claimed to have investigated everything carefully "from the beginning" in order to write an orderly account for Theophilus so that he may know the truth about the things he had been taught. When we finish reading this introduction we may not know everything Luke meant by what he wrote, but we can easily follow the main line of his thinking. We could do the same with his introduction to the book of Acts. We will skip the Gospel of John since there is not yet a consensus that its introduction ends with John 1:5.

16. *Ibid.*, p. 58.
17. John Drury, Luke, *J. B. Phillips Commentaries*, (London and Glasgow: Collins Fontana Books, 1973), p. 17.

One of the clearest introductions in the New Testament is that of the book of Hebrews. In my book, *Mark: A Twice-Told Tale*, I pointed out the elements of that introduction: 1. A succession of prophets through whom God spoke in the past, 2. A revelation in the last days, 3. Through God's Son, 4. Who is the heir, which run parallel to Mark's Parable of the Vineyard.[18] Hebrews continued:

> through whom he created the worlds. He is the reflection of God's glory and the exact imprint of God's very being, and he sustains all things by his powerful word. When he had made purification for sins, he sat down at the right hand of the Majesty on high, having become as much superior to angels as the name he has inherited is more excellent than theirs" (Heb. 1:1-4).

The circumstances surrounding the discovery of a couple of Gnostic gospels will further confirm how important a clear introduction is. Take the Gospel of Thomas, for example. In 1897 and 1903, three Greek fragments of the gospel were discovered in Egypt, the Oxyrhynchus papyri I, 654 and 655. However, because the fragments did not include the introduction or conclusion of the gospel they were not recognized as coming from that gospel. It was only after the discovery of the entire Gospel of Thomas in 1945 at Nag Hammadi, Egypt, that the two were connected. The introduction reads as follows, "These are the hidden words that the living Jesus spoke. And Didymos Judas Thomas wrote them down. And he said: 'Whoever finds the meaning of these words will not taste death.'"[19]

The case of the Gospel of Judas further illustrates the importance of an introduction for understanding a gospel. Stephen Emmel, a protégé of James Robinson, actually saw a section of the gospel that mentioned Judas, but misidentified it as a reference to Judas Didymus Thomas of the Gospel of Thomas. If he had had

---

18. Caurie Beaver, *Mark: A Twice-Told Tale*, (Eugene, Oregon: Wipf and Stock, 2009), Previously Published by Xlibris Corp., 2004), p. 238.

19. Stephen J. Patterson, and James M. Robinson, *The Fifth Gospel: The Gospel of Thomas Comes of Age*, Translated by Hans-Gebhard Bethpage et al., (Harrisburg, Pennsylvania: Trinity Press International, 1998), p. 7, and 34.

access to the introduction of the Gospel, he would have known instantly that the reference was to Judas Iscariot, Jesus' "betrayer." The introduction reads as follows, "The secret account of the revelation that Jesus spoke in conversation with Judas Iscariot during a week three days before he celebrated Passover."[20]

By clarity, I am referring to grammatical or linguistic clarity, not total interpretive clarity if these two can be distinguished. While in textual criticism the more difficult reading is usually preferred in this case, in which the expectation of clarity can be demonstrated, in my opinion, the opposite rule should apply.

When it is punctuated and translated correctly, Mark's introduction is as clear as the examples cited above. Mark's introduction should read as follows:

> The guiding principle of the good news of Jesus Christ (Son of God), as it is written in the prophet Isaiah is as follows: "See I am sending my messenger ahead of you, who will prepare your way; the voice of one crying out in the wilderness: 'Prepare the way of the Lord, Make his paths straight.'"(Mk. 1:1-3)

Using the New Oxford Annotated Bible, I have made only necessary changes: arché is translated as "(The) guiding principle" instead of "(The) beginning"; after "Son of God" I placed a comma instead of a period, and after "Make his paths straight" I placed a period instead of a comma. Finally, I added the words "is as follows" after "the prophet Isaiah" creating a completed sentence in which "(The) guiding principle" is the subject and the messenger prophecy is the predicate.

Nigel Turner pointed out that the verb "to be" was frequently omitted from the Greek sentence as it could easily be supplied by the reader. Turner even conceded that it made good sense to add the verb "to be" to the first three verses of Mark, but rejected it on statistical grounds. The translation of arché as "guiding principle"

---

20. Rodolphe Kasser, Marvin Meyer and Gregor Wurst, editors, *The Gospel of Judas from Codex Tchacos*, (Washington D. C.: National Geographic, 2006), p. 19. See also Herbert Krosney's, *The Last Gospel: The Quest for the Gospel of Judas Iscariot*, (Washington D.C.: National Geographic, 2006), p. 116.

makes the addition of the verb "to be" to this passage a viable choice.[21]

This passage, Mark 1:1–3, is the prooemium of Mark's persuasive argumentative speech, not the prologue to the gospel story of Jesus. Robert Guelich came close to this view when he separated Mark 1:1–3 from the rest of the gospel and called it a "heading."[22] Those who argue for a longer introduction for Mark (Mk. 1:1–13 or Mk. 1:1–15) base their view on the translation of arché as "beginning" and focus on Mark's story of Jesus when it began, and what it included.

In addition to the prooemium, which is an introduction to a speech, in the body of his discourse, Mark would undoubtedly have used still other Hellenistic rhetorical arguments. The next three chapters will treat in some detail the forms of these arguments beginning with the enthymeme or rhetorical syllogism.

---

21. Nigel Turner, *Grammatical Insights into the New Testament* (New York: T&T Clark International A Continuum imprint, 2004), pp. 27, 28.

22. Robert Guelich, *Mark 1–8:26*, (Dallas, Texas: Word Books, Publishers, Word Biblical Commentary, Vol. 34A, 1989), pp. 11, 12.

Chapter IV

Mark's "Simple" Rhetorical Arguments
The "for" (gar) Enthymemes

The Hellenistic Context of Jesus' Debates

BY CONTEXT I MEAN the encompassing story that enables one to understand the particular stories in Mark. Seymour Chatman in his book Story and Discourse distinguished between "story world" and "narrative world" (discourse). According to Chatman "story world" comprises all the events in a narrative arranged in absolute chronological order and "narrative world" consists of the order of events in the narrative.[1] Of course arrangement of events is only one aspect of Chatman's concept of discourse. However, I have chosen to highlight it in order to draw attention to a rather obvious consequence that follows from it: what becomes clear is that most, if not all, narratives have two beginnings and two endings, for example,[2] Mark's "narrative begins with Mark quoting God's promise to send a messenger to prepare the way of the Lord (Mark 1:1–3), but the gospel's "story world reaches all the way back to the beginning of creation" (Mk. 10:6, 13:19). Similarly, Mark's

---

1. Seymour Chatman, *Story and Discourse: Narrative Structure in Fiction and Film*, (Cornell University Press, 1972), pp. 28–29.

2. Caurie Beaver, *Mark: A Twice-Told Tale*, (Eugene, OR: Wipf and Stock Publishers, 2009), p. 169ff. Copyright 2004 by Beaver, Caurie, Previously published by Xlibris Corporation, 2004.

narrative ends with the women fleeing the empty tomb of Jesus (Mk. 16:8), but the gospel story continues up to the End of the World and coming of the Son of Man (Mk. 14:62).

Since Mark's topical references range over vast periods of time, which Thomas Mann called the "deep well of history,"[3] I will attempt to bring some semblance of order into the matter by connecting these themes with the Old Testament (the Tanak and the Septuagint). Although Mark did not portray the past as a succession of empires, as Daniel did (Dan. 7, 8),[4] it may be helpful to connect certain topics in his gospel with the various periods and cultures from which these elements ultimately derived.

In my book *Mark: A Twice-Told Tale* I already began this process by allocating the various "messianic" titles to the periods and cultures that probably gave rise to them.[5] For example, the Son of David title obviously came from Israel's Davidic royal dynasty, which ended during or shortly, after the Babylonian Exile of Judea's elite after 587 BCE. With the disappearance of the royal line, priests filled the leadership vacuum, and the "messiah" came to be thought of as a priest (Heb. 5:5–6).[6] As the Persian Empire replaces the Babylonian Empire in 539 BCE, the Jews probably

---

3. John Drury, *Tradition and Design in Luke's Gospel*, (Atlanta: John Knox Press, 1977), p. 2. First published in Great Britain in 1976 by Darton, Longman, and Todd Ltd.

4. D. S. Russell, *Daniel*, (Philadelphia: The Westminster Press, 1981), p. 116. Also Published by the Saint Andrew Press Edinburgh, Scotland. See also Edgar Hennecke's *New Testament Apocrypha* Edited by Wilhelm Schneemelcher, English translation edited by R. Mcl. Wilson, Vol. Two, p. 608. Chapter XVI Apocalyptic in Early Christianity, translated by David Hill Introduction by P. Vielhaur, who characterized this succession of empires as "Survey of History in Future-Form."

5. Caurie Beaver, *Mark: A Twice-Told Tale*, p. 215, 216. See also Gregory J. Riley, *The River of God: A History of Christian Origins*, (New York: Harper-Collins Publishers, Inc., 2001), p.11ff. Utilizing the metaphor of a river system and Stephen Jay Gould's biological evolutionary theory of punctuated equilibrium, Riley describes Israel/Judah's history not as a slow and gradual process, but one of sudden and sometimes violent changes due to contact with other cultures, separated by periods of relative stability.

6. James C. VanderKam, *The Dead Sea Scrolls Today*, (Grand Rapids, Michigan, Wm. B. Eerdmans Co., 1994), p. 117.

came under the influence of Zoroastrian eschatology, which resulted in the "messiah" being called the Son of Man (Dan. 7:13; 1 Enoch 46:1).[7] Finally, in the Hellenistic period, which began with Alexander the Great in 333 BCE, and in the Roman period after 63 BCE, the "messiah" was called the Son of God (Mk. 1:1; 15:39).[8] I have put "messiah" in quotation marks because Mark nowhere called Jesus the Messiah. Only John's gospel used the term Messiah (Jn. 1:41). Elsewhere the gospel translated Messiah into Greek as Christ (Kristos).

Mark's story of Jesus is not simply a continuation of the story of Israel in the Old Testament. The Jewish traditions were subsequently enriched by the infusion of at least three imperial cultures: Babylonian mythology, Persian Apocalyptic, and Hellenistic Rhetoric. I will begin with Hellenistic culture, which is the setting for Jesus' debates with the scribes and the source of his gospel's "simple" rhetorical arguments or enthymemes. In chapter V I will deal with apocalyptic, which is more apparent in the complex rhetorical arguments Jesus used in the debates with his opponents.

The importance of periodization cannot be over emphasized. Where a historian begins his narrative lets us in on what kind of story he will tell us. Bickerman began his story of "early" Judaism with Ezra;[9] Emil Schürer began the history of the Jewish state with the Maccabean revolt against the Syrian ruler Antiochus Epiphanes

---

7. George E. E. Nickelsburg, and James C. VanderKam, *I Enoch, A New Translation*, (Minneapolis: Fortress Press, 2004), p. 59. It is interesting to notice how Martin Hengel, who studied Hellenistic influence on the Jews expressed doubt as to "Iranian" influence on Apocalyptic, and D. S. Russell, who studied Apocalyptic, declared that there was "no doubt" that Iranian thought influenced apocalyptic. See Martin Hengel's *Judaism and Hellenism*, (Philadelphia: Fortress Press, 1974), p. 193, and D. S. Russell's *Between the Testaments*, Philadelphia: Fortress Press, 1960), p. 107.

8. For a discussion of the textual problem in Mark 1:1 see Bart D. Ehrman's *The Orthodox Corruption of Scripture*, (New York & Oxford: Oxford University Press, 1993), p. 72. Some manuscripts omit "Son of God" in Mark 1:1.

9. Elias Bickerman, *From Ezra to the Last of the Maccabees, Foundations of Post-biblical Judaism*, (New York: Schocken, 1962).

IV in the 160s BCE;[10] and Martin Hengel began his story of Judaism and Hellenism with Alexander the Great in 333 BCE.[11]

When Emil Schürer began his History of the Jewish People in the Age of Jesus Christ with the Maccabean Revolt, one could reasonably expect the following story to be one of resistance to Greek influence. Statements such as the one below tend to support this view.

> While the other oriental religions were merged in the general religious medley of the times, Judaism maintained itself essentially inviolate.[12]

By omitting the earlier period of about one hundred years of relatively peaceful Ptolemaic rule over Judea, in which Hellenistic culture took root and penetrated as far as Jerusalem, itself, Schürer left the impression—perhaps unintentionally—that the Jews resisted Greek influence from the start.[13]

---

10. Emil Schürer, *The History of the Jewish people in the age of Jesus Christ*, A New English Version Revised and Edited by Geza Vermes and Fergus Millar, Literary Editor Pamela Vernes, Organizing Editor Matthew Black, 4 Volumes, (Edinburgh: T&T Clark, Ltd., 1973). In 1961 an abridged edition of the First Division on Political history was published by Schocken Books, Inc., edited and introduced by Nahum N Glatzer. In 1972 Schocken Books published sections 32, 33, 34 of Vol. III of the Second Division on Jewish literature, also edited and introduced by Nahum N Glatzer. In the following year, 1973, the Revised English Edition appeared. There is also a single volume work by Peter Schafer on the political history of the Jews entitled The History of the Jews in the Greco-Roman world (London and New York: Routledge, Taylor and Francis Group, 2003, which began with Alexander the Great and ended with the Arab Conquests.

11. Martin Hengel, *Judaism and Hellenism* translated by John Bowden (Fortress Press, 1974). p. 2.

12. Emil Schürer, *The Literature of the Jewish People in the Time of Jesus*, Edited with an Introduction by Nahum N. Glazier (New York Schocken Books, 1972), p. 158. The Revised Edition has, "while that other Oriental religions disappeared in the general religious fusion of the time, Judaism remained essentially *unaltered*." Emil Schürer, The History of the Jewish people in the age of Jesus Christ, Vol. III.1, p. 472. It is curious to note that the name "Christ" did not appear in the abridged editions, possibly out of deference to the editor, Nahum Glatzer, who is Jewish, but reappeared on the Revised English Edition.

13. Ibid., Vol. 1, p. 125.

On the other hand Martin Hengel began his equally great study of Judaism and Hellenism with Alexander the Great and ended it with the Maccabean Revolt where Schürer's history began. By beginning with Alexander Hengel changed the narrative or story from one of resistance to Greek influence to one of acceptance of Greek culture.

By making Hellenization the main story, Hengel converted the Maccabean revolt into a subplot albeit a very important one. While Schürer wrote of the revolt in positive terms, Hengel pointed out that it had some long-range dire negative consequences. According to him what began as a domestic dispute was magnified considerably by the parties involved appealing to the Syrian ruler, Antiochus IV, and his subsequent intervening in the conflict. His meddling in a domestic dispute between "conservative" Jewish elements, who were "zealous for the law," and "hellenizers" who were "zealous against the law," led to a polarization of these two factions. The "party" zealous for the law supported the Maccabees, and overtime a certain faction became increasingly radicalized, and came to be known as the Zealots. In the two wars against Rome in the 60s and 130s C.E. Hengel says that these radical group's "zeal for the law" led to the ultimate destruction of the Jewish state.[14]

In contrast Schürer argued that it was Antiochus IV's attempt to abolish Jewish worship "that saved Judaism."[15] Schürer and Hengel are probably both right, but simply had in mind different

---

14. Martin Hengel, *Judaism & Hellenism*, p. 303–305. See also Elias Bickerman's *The God of the Maccabees: Studies on the Meaning and Origin of the Maccabean Revolt*, (Leiden: E. J. Brill, 1979), passim. He described the revolt as beginning with a domestic dispute between Jewish hellenizers and traditional Jewish factions that led to foreign intervention.

15. Emil Schürer, Vo. 1, p. 145. A final word is in order about these two great historians. In his book *Judaism and Hellenism* Hengel expressed a hope ". . .that the investigation will be extended to cover the second half of the period at a later stage," p. 1. Although he subsequently published a short work on the subject entitled *The Hellenization of Judea in the First Century after Christ* in collaboration with Christoph Markschies, originally published in 1989 by SCM Press and later by Wipf and Stock Publishers, Eugene, Oregon, it was on a much smaller scale than his first work. Perhaps Hengel's hope is fulfilled by the publication of the Revised Edition of Schürer's work.

things: Hengel was thinking of the state institutions, which *were* destroyed in the two wars with Rome, and Schürer was thinking about the religious institutions and teachings of the Pharisees, which enabled Judaism to survive as a religious community. Messianic Judaism, which is usually called Early Christianity, also survived as a religious community utilizing the same religious institutions at first and the teachings of Jesus.[16]

By now the reader may be wondering what all this has to do with Mark and Jesus. I will soon show how most of the arguments between Jesus and his opponents revolved around different interpretations of the law, the Torah, and these divergent understandings of the law sometimes had lethal consequences for the individual as well as the state. After all the Jewish leaders had to take into account this "zeal for the law," which put a sharper edge on the debates in which Jesus engaged and ultimately led to his death.

The Hellenistic Context of Mark's Rhetoric

Mark's use of a simple rhetorical argument called an enthymeme was rooted in Greek rhetoric, which was at the center of Greek education.[17] The Greek culture that accompanied Alexander the Great's rapid conquest of Palestine and other near eastern countries in the last quarter of the fourth century BCE, was like a downpour that gradually seeped in for the next three centuries.[18] To continue the metaphor the ground was prepared by a previous gradual penetration of Greek culture through travel and trade. What Alexander and his successors added was the city, and its several institutions, such as the courts, the assembly, games, and other public celebrations. The rhetorical education that supported

---

16. Caurie Beaver, *Mark: A Twice-Told Tale*, pp. 199–207.

17. H. I. Marron, *A History of Education in Antiquity*, Translated by George Lamb, (Madison, WI: University of Wisconsin Press, 1956), p. 194ff.

18. Martin Hengel, *Judaism and Hellenism, Studies in their Encounter in Palestine During the Early Hellenistic Period* (Philadelphia: Fortress Press, 1981), passim. See also Hans Jonas' *The Gnostic Religion* (Boston, Mass., Beacon Press, 1958), passim.

and perpetuated these institutions was practical in nature, and was designed to meet the legal, political, and ceremonial requirements of the community. To these three needs corresponded three types of rhetoric: judicial, deliberative, and epideictic or ceremonial. Argumentation was used in all three forms of rhetoric, which were early adapted for use by religious institutions such as the synagogue and church.

Beginning in the second century CE and continuing through the third and fourth centuries CE and even after that there was a rapprochement between Christianity and Greek philosophy. Of course, the appropriation of Greek thought to interpret the New Testament tradition became more intense as Christianity gradually ascended the social ladder. The story of this merging of Christian thought and Greek philosophical categories is told in Adolph Harnack's truly massive seven-volume *History of Dogma*.[19]

The development is usually contrasted with the New Testament period in which the exceptions recognized were the Book of Hebrews (sometimes related to Platonic thought) and the Gospel of John, a favorite gospel of the Gnostics.[20] However, Greek influence did not begin with the books that are now in the New Testament. The most important earlier examples are the Greek translation of the Old Testament, the Septuagint (LXX), which was used by most New Testament writers, and of course, the writings of Philo, a Jew, who lived in Alexandria, Egypt.

In particular, the Greek rhetorical forms of argumentation were often denied to the gospels, which were viewed as stories. William Beardslee suggested that Aristotle's *Poetics*, which dealt with narratives, should serve as a model for understanding the gospels and not Aristotle's *Rhetoric*, which dealt with public speaking in the courts, assemblies, and at public ceremonies.[21] There-

---

19. Adolph Harnack, *History of Dogma, Complete in Seven Volumes form the Third German Edition*, by Neil Buchanan, (New York: Dove Publications, Inc., 1961), passim.

20. J. N. Sanders, *the Fourth Gospel in the Early Church*, (Cambridge: The University Press, 1943), p. 47–66.

21. William A Beardslee, *Literary Criticism of the New Testament*, The New Testament Series, Ed. Dan O'Via Jr., (Philadelphia: Fortress Press, 1970), p. 4.

fore, during the last quarter of the 20th century, scholars applied literary criticism to the gospels. My own book, *Mark: A Twice-Told Tale*, was just such a work.

While it was conceded that Paul used argumentation extensively, the narrative form of the gospels constituted a barrier to allowing reasoned discourse in their case. It was the "words of the Lord," not the story of Jesus, that provided the basic principles for Paul's rational defense of the gospel. It is customary to refer to Paul's denial of an interest in the "Christ after the flesh, (II Cor. 5:16), but Gary Wills in his book, *What Paul Meant*, noted that Paul appealed to the "words of the Lord" (Jesus) a total of nine times in dealing with the various issues confronted by the churches to which he wrote. More important, his version of the Lord (Jesus's) words is earlier than their gospel counterpart when there is a parallel.[22]

To understand how Paul used a "word of the Lord" to encourage and persuade one community which had lost hope, one only needs to compare his letter to the Corinthians with that to the Thessalonians. The Corinthian community was marked by division and conflict. Paul wrote:

> For it has been reported to me by Chloe's people that there are quarrels among you, my brothers and sisters. What I mean is that each of you says, "I belong to Paul," or "I belong to Appollos," or "I belong Cephas," or "I belong to Christ." Has Christ been divided? (I Cor. 1:11–13).

Paul's solution was to recommend love as the answer to their problems. At the end of the famous hymn to love he wrote, "and now *faith*, *hope*, and *love* abide, these three, and the greatest of these is love" (I Cor. 13:13). Notice how Paul placed love in the third and final emphatic position.

However, the problem faced by the Thessalonian community was not a deficiency of love but a loss of hope in the return of the Lord. It seems that the Lord had delayed his coming so that some

---

22. Gary Wills, *What Paul Meant*, (New York: Penguin Books, 2006), pp. 45–46.

believers had died. Fear spread through the community that the deceased would not share in the benefits of the coming kingdom. There was even historical precedent for their concern, because in an early version of eschatology only the final generation enjoyed its blessings.

First, Paul commended them for their possession of what the Corinthians lacked, namely, love!

> Now concerning love of the brothers and sisters you do not need to have anyone write to you, for you yourselves have been taught by God to love one another (I Thess. 4:9).

Then Paul zeroed in on their deficiency, a loss of hope. He did so by revising his triad—faith, hope, and love—so that he placed hope in the final emphatic position. In his greeting he wrote as follows, ". . .remembering before our God and Father your work of *faith* and labor of *love* and steadfastness of *hope* in our Lord Jesus Christ" (I Thess. 1:3). Then Paul called attention to the belief in the resurrection, a belief that was absent from the earlier eschatology that focused on the final generation only, "For since we believe that Jesus died and rose again even so through Jesus, God will bring with him those who have died" (I Thess. 4:14). At this point, Paul appealed to an unspecified "word of the Lord" to support his belief that the Lord would return during his lifetime. "For this we declare to you by the word of the Lord, that we who are alive, who are left until the coming of the Lord, will by no means precede those who have died" (I Thess. 4:15). It is not just that Paul was mistaken in the belief that he would survive until the return of the Lord, but that he attributed this erroneous belief to the Lord himself. Whether by "the word of the Lord" Paul meant a saying of Jesus or a direct revelation from the Lord, it would, in either case, be problematic. In his ignorance of the time of the End, Paul is in good company because according to Mark, the Son also did not know the day or hour of the End, but only the Father (Mk. 13:32).

Mark made a similar use of the Lord (Jesus') words in his arguments and an even greater use of the stories about Jesus than Paul did. Adela Yarbro Collins wrote in her commentary on Mark, "argumentation is *generally* discursive speech, like most of the material in the letters of Paul,"[23] which seems to allow for the possibility that argumentation could sometimes take a narrative form. Then she stated flatly that the rhetoric of fiction "is still narrative, and not argumentative in form."[24] It is probably not legitimate to pit narration against argumentation. Actually, argumentation can utilize both formal reasoning and narrative representation. A story comes closest to discursive speech when it is told in the third person, and the author gives reasons for the events narrated.

Mark often used rhetorical syllogisms called enthymemes. In public speaking, the full syllogism was seldom used, since it was considered an affront to the intelligence of the audience to spell out an argument in too great a detail.[25] Instead, a speaker utilized a form of reasoning in which an unspoken premise, which he shared with audience, was combined with an observation to form a conclusion. A "simple" enthymeme consisted of a statement, "Jesus saw the disciples casting into the sea" and reason "for they were fishermen" (Mk. 1:16).

Sacred Proclamation or Rhetorical Argumentation

However, before I attempt to demonstrate this, I must first deal with formidable objections by George Kennedy an expert in the ancient rhetoric, and Robert Fowler, a Markan Scholar. According to Fowler, "Paul's rhetoric employs proofs and reasoned arguments; to an astonishing degree the Gospel of Mark eschews both."[26] Fowler also approved of Kennedy's description of the Gospel of Mark as "an example of what may be called radical

23. Adela Yarbro Collins, *Mark Hermenea Commentary*, (Minneapolis: Fortress Press, 2007), p. 90.

24. Ibid., p. 90.

25. Aristotle's *Poetics and Rhetoric*, Translated by W. Rhys Roberts in 1924, Introduction and Notes by Eugene Garver, (New York: Barnes and Noble Classics, 2005), pp. 112, 113.

26. Robert Fowler, *Let the Reader Understand: Reader-Response Criticism and the Gospel of Mark*, (Minneapolis: Fortress Press, 1991), p. 63.

Christian rhetoric, a form of 'sacred language' characterized by assertion and absolute claims of authoritative truth without evidence or logical argument."[27] Elsewhere Kennedy wrote, "when a doctrine is purely proclaimed and not couched in enthymemes, I call the technique radical Christian rhetoric. This is characteristic not only of some individual periscopes, but of entire books such as the Gospel of Mark."[28] Kennedy's description of Mark's language as "sacred language" is reminiscent of the description of New Testament Greek as a holy or sacred language before Adolf Deissmann demonstrated that New Testament authors wrote in *Koine*, the Common Hellenistic Greek of the day.[29]

A little later, Kennedy defines an enthymeme:

> Deductive proof in rhetoric is called the enthymeme. An enthymeme commonly takes the form of a statement and a supporting reason as in "Blessed are the poor in spirit (statement), for theirs is the kingdom of heaven" (reason) (Matt. 5:3).

He then exhibited the full form of the implied syllogism:

> Major Premise: those who receive the kingdom of heaven are blessed.
> Minor Premise: The poor in spirit will receive the kingdom of heaven.
> Conclusion: Thus, the poor in spirit are blessed.[30]

Kennedy even allowed that Mark contained enthymemes, but minimized their importance by describing them as "of a very simple sort."[31] What he failed to notice was the overwhelming

---

27. George Kennedy, *New Testament Interpretation through Rhetorical Criticism*, (Chapel Hill and London: University of North Carolina Press, 1984), p. 104.

28. Ibid., p. 7.

29. Adolph Deismann, *Light from the Ancient East*, (Grand Rapids, Michigan: Baker Book House, 1978), passim.

30. George Kennedy, *New Testament Interpretation through Rhetorical Criticism*, p. 16.

31. Ibid., p. 105.

number of such "simple" enthymemes in Mark. In the index to Taylor's commentary are listed over 60 instances of the use of the word 'for,' which usually forms an enthymeme.[32] There is at least one in every chapter of Mark, and they range in number from one, in chapter 2, to eight in chapter 6.

It is notable that they occur at important junctures in Mark's speech: at the call of Jesus' first two disciples, "Jesus saw Simon and Andrew casting into the sea (statement) for they were fishermen (reason)(Mk. 1:16); at the stilling of the storm on the sea, the disciples were amazed (statement) for they did not understand about the loaves (reason)(Mk. 6:52);[33] at the transfiguration Peter suggested to Jesus that they build dwellings for Jesus, Moses, and Elijah (statement) "for he did not know what to say." (reason)(Mk. 9:5, 6); and finally when the women fled the empty tomb of Jesus Mark said that they said nothing to anyone for they were afraid (Mk. 16:8).

After he translated Aristotle's *Rhetoric*, Kennedy may have been willing to reconsider his previously expressed views on Mark's use of enthymemes. In the preface he asserted that:

---

32. Vincent Taylor, *The Gospel According to St. Mark*, (MacMillan's St. Martin's Press, 1966), p. 675. They are as follows, "i. 16, 22, 38, ii. 15, iii, 10, 21, iv. 22, 25, v. 8, 28, 42, vi. 14, 17, 18, 20, 31, 48, 50, 52, vii. 3, 10, 21, 27, viii. 35, 36, 37, 38, ix. 6 bis, 31, 34, 39, 40, 41, 49, x. 14, 22, 27, 45, xi. 13, 18 bis, 32, xii. 12, 14, 23, 25, 44, xiii. 8, 11, 19, 22, 33, 35, xiv. 2, 5, 7, 40, 56, 70, xv. 10, 14, xvi, 4, 8 bis." See also Richard B Vinson's "A Comparative Study of the Use of Enthymemes in the Synoptic Gospels" published in *Persuasive Artistry: Studies in New Testament Rhetoric in Honor of George A. Kennedy*, edited by Duane F. Watson (copyright 1991 by Sheffield Academic Press, Published by JSOT, an imprint of Sheffield Academic Press Ltd, The University of Sheffield, Sheffield, England), pp. 119–141.

Vinson's count of Mark's enthymemes is 77. The difference between Vinson's count and Taylor's is at least partially explained by the former's inclusion of *hoti*, which means the same as gar. However, Vinson does not relate Mark's enthymemes to the larger argumentative structure of that gospel. For Vinson gar (for) is primarily a matter of narrative style.

33. Quentin Quesnell, *The Mind of Mark Interpretation and Method through the Exegesis of 6:52*, (Rome: Pontifical Biblical Institute, 1969), passim. Quesnell's entire book is about this "simple" enthymeme.

A major doctrine of the *Rhetoric* is the use of the enthymeme, or rhetorical syllogism. In Aristotle's own writing enthymemes often take the form of a statement followed by a clause introduced by the Greek particle, gar (for), which gives a supporting reason or sometimes a corollary. These occur on every page but are often obscured by other translators. I have kept them, using a semicolon and the English particle "for" as a way of drawing them to the attention of the reader and making the device familiar.[34]

Nor did Kennedy any longer call them "simple" enthymemes in Aristotle. What Kennedy said about the importance of the "gar" enthymemes in Aristotle's *Rhetoric* could also be said about Mark's use of the same rhetorical device.

Bird's Article: "Some Gar Clauses in St. Mark's Gospel"

In 1953, C. H. Bird did a very interesting study of nine "gar" clauses in the Gospel of Mark.[35] According to Bird, Mark's use of the "gar" clauses is allusive in nature and suggests a richer meaning than their plain logic would indicate if taken literally. The enthymeme

---

34. George Kennedy, *Aristotle's Rhetoric on a Theory of Civic Discourse Newly Translated with Introduction, Notes and Appendices*, (New York & Oxford, Oxford University Press, 1991), p. xii.
   Even after translating Aristotle, Kennedy did not reconsider his view of Mark. Again, he accepted the theory of that gospel current in his day. While as an expert of rhetoric, he recognized the prominence of the gar (for) enthymeme in Aristotle's, he failed to see it in Mark. See *Words Well Spoken: George Kennedy's Rhetoric of the New Testament* edited by C. Clifton Black, and Deeane F. Watson, published by Baylor University Press, Waco, Texas, 2008), Afterword by George A. Kennedy, p. 187.

35. C. H. Bird, "Some *gar* clauses in St. Mark's Gospel," J. T. S., 4 (1953), 171–87, *Journal of Theological Studies*. See also Janice Capel Anderson and Stephen D. Moore, editors, *Mark and Method*, (Minneapolis: Fortress Press, 1992, p. 119. Anderson noted four gar (for) arguments in the story of John the Baptist's death (Mk. 6:14, 17, 18, 20) and called it "a typical narrative device in Mark," but failed to analyze it as a logical argument and determine its function in a rational discourse or persuasive speech.

about the disciples casting nets into the sea, for they were fishermen (Mk. 1:16, 17) alluded to Jesus' promise that he would make them fishers of men. Also, the enthymeme about the barren fig tree yielded no fruit for it was not the season for figs (Mk. 11:13) alluded to the imminent destruction of the Temple as the interpolation of Jesus' cleansing of the Temple would suggest. We now have an entire book on this "simple" enthymeme and the "sandwich" construction in which it occurs entitled *The Barren Temple* and *the Withered Tree* by W. Telford.

One of Bird's more interesting interpretations has to do with the story of the raising of Jairus' daughter. When Jesus raised her, Mark wrote, "and immediately the little girl arose and walked for (gar) she was twelve years old" (Mk. 5:42). It is obvious that her age alone is not the reason for her walking. The RSV got rid of the problem by dropping the subordinating causal particle gar (for) and placing the offending clause in a parenthesis.

And immediately the girl got up and began to walk about (she was twelve years of age)" (Mk. 5:42). The Greek has because or "for she was twelve years of age."

Bird concluded that the difficulty gave him permission to interpret the story symbolically. In my book *Mark: A Twice-Told Tale* I argued that it is legitimate to use allegorical interpretation only where an author signals that he intended what he wrote to be read allegorically. The number 12 used in the story of Jairus' daughter and the interpolated story of the woman healed of an illness that she had suffered from for 12 years are just such indicators.

Bird observed that Jairus daughter represented the "New Israel," because she was fruitful, having just entered childbearing age, but he failed to notice that the interpolated story of the older woman, who was "healed" of her menstruation, became unfruitful and a fitting symbol of the "Old Israel." However, none of Bird's observations cancels the enthymeme form of these sayings; they merely illustrate Mark's creative use of this type of rhetorical argument. However, even Bird did not seem to be aware of how pervasive this "simple" argument was in the Gospel of Mark.

Responses to Bird's View

While surveying the influence of Bird's view, I arrived at the following observations about the gar (for) clauses. These definitions did not guide the following study, but grew out of it. However, they are placed here to guide the reader—the order of discovery is not always the order of presentation. Our descriptive definition of the *gar* (for) clauses consists of three parts:

1. Grammatically the gar construction is *a dependent clause* introduced by the causal particle, "for" (*gar*).

2. Functionally, the *gar* clause is frequently a parenthesis, which interrupts and comments on the surrounding story.

3. And formally, the gar clause often forms *an enthymeme* or rhetorical argument used in speeches.

According to Margaret Thrall, Bird attempted to derive allusions to the Old Testament from the meaning of the word *gar* (for), which means what it does in English, namely, because. She denied that the word *gar* had any additional allusive meaning, and claimed that such references to the Old Testament, ". . . must be deduced from the material content of the *gar* clauses and their total context, and not from the fact that *gar* is the introductory particle."[36] Thrall is probably correct both in what she denied and what she asserted, because the meaning of any word or phrase is determined by its context.

However, I must take exception to Thrall's comment about Mark's overuse of the word gar when she wrote,

> Writers who use *gar* frequently, as Mark does, are not always logical thinkers who develop an argument stage by stage, representing each further statement as the necessary deduction from the previous one, or who tell a story in strict chronological sequence, with every detail in its logical position in the narrative.[37]

---

36. Margaret E. Thrall, *Greek Particles in the New Testament*, (Grand Rapids, Michigan: Wm. B. Eerdmans, 1962), p. 50. See also pp. 41–50.

37. Ibid., p. 47.

Thrall is apparently contrasting Mark with a scientific essay in which more formal reasoning is used, and narrative, types of literature in which temporal sequence is used. But Mark is neither of these. It is a persuasive speech for which Aristotle recommended the use of the rhetorical argument introduced by the word gar,[38] and Aristotle, who practically invented logic, could hardly be described as a "not always logical thinker." A comment of Nigel Turner would also suggest that the Gospel of Mark is a speech that was first delivered orally and then written down. Concerning Mark's use of parentheses he wrote,

> Sometimes parenthesis involves the interjection of a whole sentence—not a word or two—into the heart of another sentence. It is characteristic of speakers rather than writers—a writer has more opportunity to revise his work and smooth out avoidable interjections—and we observe that St. Paul fell into the habit, perhaps because he made a practice of dictating letters to a scribe."[39]

The editorial (redaction) critic, E. J. Pryke, accepted Thrall's criticism of Mark's use of gar.[40] As an editorial (redaction) critic Pryke was primarily interested in separating tradition from editorial additions in Mark. It is interesting that he assigned 57 of the gar clauses to Mark, the editor, and only 6 to his sources.[41]

While editorial (redaction) critics distinguished between sources/traditions and editorial additions, Fowler, a reader-response critic, distinguish between the narrative, what the characters in the story are doing and saying, and the discourse, what the author is saying about the story. Through such commentary the author instructs the reader as to how he is to interpret the story.

---

38. *Aristotle On Rhetoric: A Theory of Civic Discourse, Newly Translated with Introduction, Notes, and Appendices by George A. Kennedy*, (New York and Oxford: Oxford University Press, 1991), pp. 186–87.

39. Nigel Turner, *Grammatical Insights into the New Testament*, (London & New York: T&T Clark International, A Continuum imprint, 2004), p. 64.

40. E. J. Pryke, *Redactional Style in the Marcan Gospel*, (Cambridge: Cambridge University Press, 1978, pp. 126–127 n.4.

41. Ibid., p. 135.

According to Fowler,

> Mark frequently uses gar to offer explanatory, parenthetical remarks on the story. Critics often note Mark's peculiar usage of gar clauses, which almost always take on the appearance of an awkward afterthought; that is, the gar parenthesis almost always follows an element of the narrator's exposition that it should logically precede.[42]

Here Fowler appears to be accepting Thrall's criticism of Mark mediated through Pryke's work as Fowler mentioned the latter but not the former.[43]

This criticism of Mark by Thrall and Fowler ignores the formulaic character of enthymemes and Aristotle's advice to use them in speeches in which full syllogisms would put the audience to sleep or to flight. Under the heading "Parenthetical Comments" Fowler briefly discussed sixteen gar clauses.[44]

However, Fowler's separation of story and discourse makes more sense than editorial critics distinction between Mark's sources and his editorial additions, because, except for Old Testament quotations,[45] we do not have Mark's sources, and the attempt to reconstruct them from that gospel has not been successful.

---

42. Robert M. Fowler, *Let the Reader Understand*, (Minneapolis: Fortress Press, 1991), pp. 92–93.

43. Robert M. Fowler, *Loaves and Fishes*, (Chico, CA: Scholars Press, Society of Biblical Literature, 1981), p. 207 n. 82.

44. Robert M. Fowler, *Let the Reader Understand*, pp. 92–98.

45. C. Clifton Black, *The Disciples according to Mark: Markan Redaction in Current Debate*, (Grand Rapids, Michigan: Wm .B. Eerdmans Publishing Co., 2012), p. 317. In the case of the Old Testament quotations in Mark we can observe how that gospel edited and understood the Scriptures. Black's evaluation of redaction, or Editorial criticism is based on Robert Stein's criteria for uncovering Mark's editorial work. Then he followed up with a detailed study of three redaction (editorial) critical works: a conservative Robert P. Meye's, *Jesus and the Twelve*, a moderate ("mediate") Ernest Best's, *Following Jesus*, and a liberal Theodore J. Weeden's, *Mark—Traditions in Conflict*. I agree with Black's conclusion that any contribution editorial critics made to our understanding of Mark—and they did make some—was not due to their pursuit of their avowed method, but was a result of their departure from it.

Editorial critics have made valuable contributions to the study of Mark but not due to their method.

A final and sympathetic example of editorial critics' uptake of Bird's article is that of Telford's book *the Barren Temple and the Withered Tree*. In my opinion, Telford correctly placed Bird among the scholars who take Mark to be ". . .a theologian, the creative author of a symbolic and highly allusive gospel. Profounder meanings lie behind the arrangement and redaction of his material. In particular Mark's frequent and enigmatic *gar* clauses (usually omitted by Matthew and Luke) are indicators, Bird suggests, of his 'allusive' method."[46] It goes beyond our purpose here to discuss in detail this valuable work, which deals with Old Testament and Rabbinic sources thoroughly.

In his book The Mind of Mark Quentin Quesnell took up the challenge of interpreting one gar clause in that gospel, "and they were utterly astounded, for (gar) they did not understand about the loaves, but their hearts were hardened" (Mk. 6:52). He did so by placing the clause in four successive contexts.[47]

1. In the immediate context Jesus came to his disciples walking on the water. Mark says the disciples were amazed and dumbfounded because or for they failed to understand something about the loaves with which Jesus had just fed 5000 people (Mk. 6:45–52).

2. The wider context contains multiple references to breads and misunderstanding (Mk. 6:3—8:21). In my opinion the key to the meaning of the references to the bread has to do with the fact that the bread was broken. The Syrophoenician woman referred to the crumbs under the table that feed the dogs. After the subsequent feeding of the four thousand, Jesus called attention to the baskets of bread fragments picked up by the disciples after the two crowds were fed (Mk. 8:19–27). Finally,

46. William R. Telford, *The Barren Temple and the Withered Tree*, (Sheffield Published by JSOT Press, Department of Biblical Studies, The University of Sheffield, 1980), p. 20.

47. Quentin Quesnell, *The Mind of Mark Interpretation and Method through the Exegesis of 6:52*, (Rome: Pontifical Biblical Institute, 1969), pp. 58-88.

at the Last Supper Jesus explained that the broken bread was his body (Mk. 14:22). In my book *Mark: A Twice-Told Tale* I discussed this subject in much greater detail.[48]

3. The third context is the Gospel as a whole, which takes us beyond our purpose. Enough has been written to illustrate the importance of context for interpreting the gar clauses.

4. Passing over Mark's Jewish and Hellenistic settings Quesnell calls attention to a fourth context, the Christian thought-world, which takes us beyond Mark altogether.

Quesnell did not mention Bird's article possibly because Bird did not discuss the gar clause at Mark 6:52. Nor did Quesnell mention Aristotle or the Greek term for the gar clause, enthymeme.

The final piece of the puzzle presented by the gar clauses was put in place by George Kennedy's cross-disciplinary study entitled New Testament through Rhetorical Criticism. The puzzle consists of three parts: Grammatically the gar construction is a dependent clause introduced by a causal particle, which in English is *for* or *because*, functionally it is an explanatory clause instructing the reader or hearer as to how to read or interpret the story, and formally it is an enthymeme or rhetorical argument used in a speech.[49]

The best description of rhetorical arguments and their relationship to scientific arguments, syllogisms, and their application to the study of Mark is found in Mary Ann Tolbert's *Sowing the Gospel*.[50] She referred both to Kennedy's work and Aristotle's *Rhetoric*, but did not discuss the "simple" gar clauses at length. Nor did she mention Bird's article. Her main contribution to our subject is a very valuable discussion of some of the more complex

---

48. Caurie Beaver, *Mark: A Twice-Told Tale*, pp. 137-51.

49. George A. Kennedy, *New Testament Interpretation through Rhetorical Criticism*, p. 7.

50. Mary Ann Tolbert, *Sowing the Gospel, Mark's World in Literary-Historical Perspective*, (Minneapolis: Augsburg Press, 1989), pp. 250-56.

enthymemes or rhetorical arguments employed by Jesus in his debates with his opponents.

Old Israel versus New Israel: Sects in the Second Temple Period

In the second temple period each "sect" struggled to establish itself as the "true" or "New Israel" in contrast to the "false" or "Old Israel." Other Markan images for this notion were the new patch (New Israel) on an old garment (Old Israel), and new wine in old wine skins (Mk. 2:21–22). According to Thomas A. Thompson, this rhetorical argument is one of the keys to the *Tanak* (Old Testament), and is an organizing principle in its composition. Mark's gospel is just a more recent example of this argumentative device designed to establish the legitimacy of his messianic Jewish community. Thompson wrote:

> The past is a scene of failure ever to be overcome by a "New Israel" that will finally follow God's will for them. It is a story, not of biblical faith, but of human apostasy. Such a story demands a rejection of the past and a reorientation to a new future. It is this future orientation of the idealistic concept of "New Israel" that marks the self-identity of the bearers of the tradition.[51]

A little later Thompson explained how this notion shaped the biblical tradition:

> They understood their sources and presented them as traditions of "Old Israel." The coherence and meaning that they gave to these traditions did not reflect the past, that is, the actual relations of events among groups and individuals of the early Iron Age. It reflected and answered rather the needs of the writers and their audiences, who centuries later, developed a world-view in which commitments to a moral and philosophical life dominated. In this view, Old Israel and its traditions of

---

51. Thomas A. Thompson, *The Mythic Past: Biblical Archaeology and the Myth of Israel* (New York: Basic Books, 1999), p. 25.

the past represented human failure. It was an example of error and sin. The tradition was important as warning , and it defined the listeners' hopes in the commitment to a "New Israel" of their own lives and of their own future. That is how the tradition made sense for them.[52]

What Thompson wrote could serve as a commentary on the older woman (Old Israel) and Jairus daughter (new Israel). According to Peter Ellis, this theme of the "Old Israel" versus the "New Israel" was also prominent in the Gospel of Matthew. In the case of Mark, the Temple authorities and the crowd were the "Old Israel" and Mark's community, the "New Israel"; for Matthew, Jamnian Judaism was the "Old Israel" and the Matthean Community was the "New Israel:"

> Matthew's ecclesiology is characterized by its claim that the true Israel is to be found, not in Jamnian Judaism led by the Pharisees, but in the Christian church.[53]

In the next chapter I will deal with the complex rhetorical arguments of Jesus' debates, beginning with a brief sketch of the cosmic context in which they occur.

---

52. Ibid., p. 68.

53. Peter F. Ellis, *Matthew: His Mind and His Message*, (Collegeville, Minnesota, The Liturgical Press, 1974), p. 114.

Chapter V

Complex Rhetorical Arguments
Mark's Account of Jesus' Debates

The Cosmic Context of the Debates

MARY ANN TOLBERT POINTED out that while the form of Mark's arguments is Hellenistic, the content is Jewish;[1] I would add a "Jewish" heavily influenced by at least three earlier Imperial cultures, the Babylonian, Persian and Greek. Having dealt with the Hellenistic (Greek) context, I will now consider the contribution of the other two previous world empires. Once again I will allow Mark's story-world references to guide me. In his argument against the permissibility of divorce Jesus referred to the "beginning (arché) of creation (Mk. 10:12). The Pharisees argued that Moses permitted divorce, but Jesus pointed out that it was a concession due to the hardness of their hearts, but from the "beginning of creation" God joined male and female together and no man was allowed to separate them. To explain how Jesus could draw a principle from the creation story in a legal argument one must understand the nature and purpose of the creation account in Genesis (Gen. 1:1—9:17).

---

1. Mary Ann Tolbert, *Sowing the Gospel*, (Minneapolis: Fortress Press, 1989), pp. 250.

From Gods to Elements:
The Creation of the Physical Universe

In Genesis 1:1 the King James Version of the Bible reads,

> In the beginning God created the heaven and the earth.

But Genesis 1:2, 3 reads,

> and the earth was without form, and void; and darkness was upon the face of the deep. And the Spirit of God moved upon the face of the waters. Then God said, "Let there be light;" and there was light.

The problem arises from the circumstance that after God created the heaven and the earth in Genesis 1:1, in Genesis 1:2, 3 the earth was still a dark, shapeless and empty watery abyss. To explain this "contradiction" some fundamentalists advocate a so-called "gap" theory which maintains that in Genesis 1:1 God created the heaven and the earth in the remote past after which the earth underwent a catastrophic destruction not unlike the flood in Noah's day. This hypothetical "gap" enabled them to accommodate the vast geological ages discovered by science.[2] The late Harvard evolutionary biologist Stephen Jay Gould referred to the "gap" theory as a reconciliationist approach to the problem of the relation of Genesis and geology.[3]

Unfortunately, the gap theory is based on a mistranslation of Genesis 1:1–3. The King James Version translated Genesis 1:1 as a complete sentence,

> In the beginning God created the heaven and the earth.

---

2. *The Scofield Reference Bible*, Edited by Rev. C. I. Scofield, (New York: Oxford University Press, 1945), p. 3n2. See also Henry H. Halley's *Halley's Bible Handbook*, (Grand Rapids, Michigan: Zondervan Publishing House, 1965), p. 59. See also Henry H. Halley's *Deluxe Edition Halley's Bible Handbook*, (Grand Rapids, Michigan, 2007), p. 86.

3. Stephen Jay Gould, *I Have Landed: The End of a Beginning in Natural History*, (New York: Three Rivers Press, 2003), pp. 138, 139.

But Hebrew scholars point out that it is a dependent clause, which the New Revised Standard Version translated as,[4]

> In the beginning when God created the heavens and the earth, the earth was a formless void and darkness covered the face of the deep, while a wind from God swept over the face of the waters. Then God said, "Let there be light;" and there was light (Gen. 1:1-3).

What this translation reveals is a number of things that God did not create: the void, the darkness, the shapeless earth, the wind (air), the waters (water), and probably the light (fire). This would imply that God did not create out of nothing (creation ex nihilo),[5] but rather used pre-existing materials, namely, the four elements of ancient science, which were common to the Babylonians,[6] Greeks,[7] and others: earth, air, water and fire.

---

4. Mark S. Smith, *The Priestly Vision of Genesis 1*, (Minneapolis: Fortress Press, 2010), pp. 43ff. He has a very thorough discussion of the Hebrew terms and the many issues involved. See also the discussion in the *HarperCollins Study Bible*, General Editor Harold W. Attridge, (HarperCollins Publishers, 2006), p. 5.

5. *Ibid*. In other words, creation did not consist in calling things into existence, but in ordering and arranging pre-existing materials. Mark Smith dealt in detail with the one apparent exception to this rule,: when God said, "Let there be light; and there was light," he appeared to be creating it out of nothing. However, this phrase, when used elsewhere, God is using available materials. Smith makes a good case for considering the light as pre-existing as God's essence. When he said, "Let there be light," he is simply making it visible, just as he said ". . . let the dry land appear" (Gen. 1:9). See also Loren R. Fisher, "From Chaos to Cosmos," *Encounter 26* (1965), p. 184.

6. Hermann Gunkel, *Creation and Chaos in the Primeval Era and the Eschaton*, Trans. by K. William Whitney Jr., (Grand Rapids, Michigan/Cambridge, UK: William B. Eerdman Publishing Company, 2006). A classical work that is still worth reading.

7. A very thorough study of the presocratics is W. K. C. Guthries, *A History of Greek Philosophy, Vol. I: The Earlier Presocratics and the Pythagoreans* (London, New York, Melbourne, Cambridge: Cambridge University Press, 1962), passim, and *Vol. II: The Presocratic Tradition from Parmenides to Democrites*, (Cambridge University Press, 1965). A still valuable classical work on the Presocratics is John Burnet's *Early Greek Philosophy*, (Cleveland and New York: Meridian Books, The World Publishing Company, 1965; First edition published April 1892).

This issue gave rise to a minor controversy between Delitzsch and Gunkel, two Old Testament scholars. Delitzsch had claimed that Genesis 1 did not assert that God created everything, because it did not explain the origin of "chaos." Gunkel's reply that the author of Genesis 1 would have wanted to express the idea that "God is the almighty creator of heaven and earth," if only he had thought the matter through to a conclusion is very weak. The new translation of Genesis 1:1 agrees with Delitzsch not Gunkel![8] However, Gunkel's notion that Genesis 1 stems from Babylonian traditions because of their common notion of a struggle with floodwaters is sound.[9]

Two facts seem to distinguish the Genesis creation story from the Babylonian one: the apparent absence of mythological elements and the lack of a combat myth. However, upon closer inspection both facts may be found to be present in Genesis. Because the Priestly author of the Genesis creation story attributed all creative activity directly to God, his account appears less mythological than its Babylonian counterpart, in which the creation results from a battle between the gods. However, appearance can be deceptive. After all in Genesis 1 the creation was accomplished by God's verbal commands: "Let there be light" (Gen. 1:3), "Let there be a dome" (Gen. 1:6), "Let the dry land appear" (Gen. 1:9), "Let the earth put forth vegetation" (Gen. 1:11). Creation by verbal command presupposes that the elements so addressed,

---

8. Hermann Gunkel, *Israel and Babylon*, Translated by E. S. B. and K. C. Hanson, (Cascade Books, Eugene, OR: Wipf and Stock Publishers, 2009), p. 22.

9. Hermann Gunkel, *Creation and Chaos in the Primeval Era and the Eschaton*, pp. 11, 12. The creation and flood stories may have come to the attention of Judea's elite during the Babylonian Exile. However, they could also have learned of these traditions from the Assyrians earlier. After writing about Assyria's legal, military, and technological accomplishments, Trawick asserted that, "Their main contribution did not consist of creative or practical works, however, but rather of the transmission of Sumerian and Babylonian culture to the Persians, Greeks and Romans."

Buckner B. Trawick, *The Bible as Literature: the Old Testament and the Apocrypha*, (New York, Evanston, San Francisco, London: Barnes & Noble Books: A Division of Harper & Row Publishers, 1970), p. 4. See also Baruch Halpern's "The Assyrian Astronomy of Genesis 1 and the Birth of Milesian Philosophy" originally published in *Eretz Israel 27* (Fs. Hayim and Miriam Tadmar, 2003), pp. 427, 442.

understood and obeyed God's commands. Mark cast Jesus in the role of the creator when he had him rebuke the wind and calm the sea (Mk. 4:39). When Jesus stilled the storm, his disciples asked, "who then is this, that even the wind and the sea obey him?" (Mk. 4:41). One is reminded of God's sending of the wind over the waters in Genesis (Gen. 1:2).

The pre-Socratics carried the process of "demythologizing" one step further by explaining creation as due to the interaction of the natural elements: earth, air, fire, and water. They even superseded this essentially meteorological model of creation by searching for a single element to explain the virtually endless transformations in nature. At first they chose the four elements one after the other,[10] and then postulated a more basic substance, the atom, not identical with any of the four elements. Until modern times this substance was considered indivisible, the atom (a = not and tom = split).[11]

The Genesis account of creation falls between the Babylonian and Greek views, but is closer to the former. It only remains to be shown that the combat myth is also present in Genesis. While the Babylonian combat myth featuring a battle between Marduk (the god of Babylon) and Tiamat (the god of the chaotic flood waters) preceded the creation of the universe and man,[12] in Genesis the combat followed the creation and was between God and Man. Of course, the serpent led men to sin (Gen. 3:1), and the sons of God married the daughters of men and further corrupted mankind (Gen. 6:1-8) leading to the resurgence of the flood waters controlled at creation. Setting the two passages side by side removes any doubt that the flood story belong together with the creation story,

---

10. W. K. C. Guthrie, *A History of Greek Philosophy, Vol. I: The Earlier Presocratics and the Pythagoreans* In this volume Guthrie discusses this process beginning with Thales choice of water as the primary element, Anaximande choice of the "Unlimited," Anaximenes air, and Heraclitus fire.

11. John Burnet, *Early Greek Philosophy*, p. 53.

12. *The Ancient Near East, Vol. I, An Anthology of Texts and Picture*, Edited by James B. Pritchard, (New Jersey: Princeton University Press, 1958), pp. 31-39.

> ... while a wind from God swept over the face of the waters (Gen. 1:2)
>
> And God made a wind blow over the earth, and the waters subsided; (Gen. 8:1)

After reasserting control over his creation following Noah's flood, God hung up his war (rain)bow in the sky just as Marduk after defeating Tiamat, places a similar sign in the sky. Here I am following the views of Bernard F. Batto, who claimed that the Priestly author of Genesis extended the creation story through the flood story. Only then was the creation complete with the final victory of God over the primeval ocean.[13]

The Rule or Reign of God: The Creation of the Justice System

Alan M. Dershowitz, a Harvard law professor, gave a unique perspective on the Genesis creation account. In a book on Genesis he referred to a question raised by Rashi, a medieval Jewish commentator: why does a creation story introduce a book of laws? He then broadened the question to ask why a law book would contain any stories at all. He argued that the stories are needed to illustrate the need for the rules by showing that men were doing what the rules forbade; there would be no need for a law against murder unless men had committed murder. Hence the story of Cain and Abel (Gen. 4:8). Therefore, I agree with Dershowitz that laws grow out of experience that is recorded in stories.[14]

However, I would argue that the creation story had still another function. Its main thrust was to establish the rule or reign of God by setting up His government and justice system by which the laws could be administered. To accomplish this God delegated

---

13. Bernard F. Batto, *Mythmaking in the Biblical Tradition, Slaying the Dragon*, (Louisville, Kentucky: Westminster/John Knox Press, 1992). Chapter 3 "The Priestly Revision of the Creation Myth" is indispensable for understanding the creation story in Genesis.

14. Alan M. Dershowitz, *The Genesis of Justice*, (New York, NY: Warner Books, A Time Warner Company, 2000), p. 217ff.

the authority to rule the heavens to the personified astral bodies, the sun, moon and stars (Gen. 1:14–18), and the authority to rule the earth to man (Gen. 1:26–28). This view of the priority of creation to the laws is confirmed by an early Jewish saying attributed to Joshua ben Korkha in 150 CE, ". . .'the yoke of the divine sovereignty' . . . must be assumed prior to 'the yoke of the commandments'. . ."[15]

What is surprising about this delegated authority to rule is that it was granted to man as such and not to a king or even to a priest. This may have been due to the circumstance that the creation story was composed during the Babylonian Exile when there was no reigning Jewish King. Besides it would not have been "politically correct" to have God delegate authority to rule to a King or priest because the Jews lived under the rule of the empires, the Babylonian and later the Persian. Meanwhile there was a shift from rule by Kings' decrees to rule by the Torah interpreted by scribes. Priests continued to exercise cultic authority (once the Temple was rebuilt), and executive functions under the direction of foreign rulers,[16] but Judicial determinations came into the hands of professional scribes and teachers of the Torah. According to Bickerman during this period learned argument superseded authoritative decree. Royal rule was not re-established until the second century BCE by the Maccabees.[17]

---

15. Gustaf Dalman, *The Words of Jesus: Considered in the Light of Post Biblical Jewish Writings and the Aramaic Language*, Translated by D.M. Kay, (Eugene, OR: Wipf and Stock Publishers, 1997), pp. 97, 98. See also Loren R. Fisher, "Creation at Ugarit and in the Old Testament." *V.T. 15* (1965), pp. 313–316. He discusses creation as rule. Jennifer M. Dines in an article entitled "Creation Under Control: Power Language in Genesis 1:1—2:3" published in *Studies in the Greek Bible: Essays in honor of Francis T. Gignac, S.J.* Ed. by Jeremy Corley and Vincent Skemp, Catholic Biblical Quarterly Monograph Series, 44, pp. 1ff. She discussed God's delegation of authority to rule in terms of Kingship, but did not explain why the authority appears to have been delegated to man as such and not to the king or priest in Gen. 1.

16. James A. Sanders, *Torah and Canon*, Eugene, OR: Wipf and Stock Publishers, 1999), p. 49. Previously published by Fortress Press, 1972.

17. Elias Bickerman, *From Ezra to the Last of the Maccabees, Foundations of Post-biblical Judaism*, (New York: Schocken Books, 1962), p. 18.

Complex Rhetorical Arguments

The Torah gave rise to divergent interpretations, which in turn spawned a number of sects: Pharisees, Sadducees, Essenes, and the Jesus sect. This diversity of interpretation is true of any written law book, such as our own constitution, which also produced different interpretations and led to various political parties. Dershowitz described this contentious setting in the following colorful words:

> The Talmud preserves dissenting views for posterity; the midrash has people arguing with angels, angels arguing with God and everybody arguing with each other.[18]

Such was the argumentative setting in which Jesus' debates with his opponents took place. In this competitive environment even Jesus and Mark were obliged to give reasons for their opinions. Hence, the numerous enthymeme (rhetorical arguments) which make a statement followed by a reason for the assertion, and the more complex enthymemes that resulted from the give and take of the debates. Dershowitz pointed to a similar form in the Torah, which he called a "motive clause," in which a rule is given followed by a reason for keeping it.[19] A detailed study of this form is found in Rifat Sonsino's motive Clauses in Hebrew Law.[20]

The Cosmic World View of Apocalyptic: Common Ground for the Debates in Mark

In dealing with the Persian Period and Apocalyptic once again I will begin with a Markan reference to his story-world. When Mark wrote about the Tribulation, a troubled time that was to come just before the End of the world, again he used the phrase "from (the) beginning of creation,"

---

18. Alan M. Dershowitz, *The Genesis of Justice*, p. 221.

19. *Ibid.*, p. 220.

20. Rifat Sonsino, *Motive Clauses in Hebrew Law*, (Chico, CA: Scholars Press, Society of Biblical Literature, 1980).

For in those days there will be suffering, such as has not been from the beginning of creation, no, and never will be (Mk. 13:19).

Unlike the Gospel of John, which referred to the beginning of time (Jn. 1:1),[21] Mark referred to the beginning of the series of God's creative activities. It may have been no accident that Mark's focus on this time of affliction before the End of the World took his mind back to the beginning of creation. It should lead one to wonder whether there was a relationship between the tribulation and something in the creation story in Genesis. If in Mark's view the Kingdom of God was ushered in by a period of intense suffering, according to Batto the completion of the original creation in Noah's day was also preceded by a period of great destruction, the Flood in which God's rule was brought about through great conflict,[22] suffering, and death.

However, the Babylonian Creation myth was not a suitable model for understanding, the prolonged conflicts of Israel's history. Once Marduk won the battle against Tiamat, all opposition was silenced and the order established was intended to last forever. By adding the flood story to the creation story, the Priestly author of Genesis opened up the possibility of adopting a better model for the understanding of the ongoing battles of history found in the Zoroastrian religion.[23] There the victory came after a long struggle between Ahura Mazda and Ahriman in which humans participated resulting in the eventual triumph of good over evil.[24]

When Jesus proclaimed that the Kingdom of God was at hand, he was repeating the main theme of the Genesis creation story, namely, the establishment of God's Kingdom or rule. However,

---

21. "In the beginning was the Word, and the Word was with God, and the Word was God." (Jn. 1:1)

22. Bernard F. Batto, *Slaying the Dragon*, p. 87. See also Loren R. Fisher, *From Chaos to Cosmos*, p. 186.

23. Bernard F. Batto, *Slaying the Dragon*, p. 85.

24. John J Collins, *The Apocalyptic Imagination, AN Introduction to the Jewish Matrix of Christianity*, (New York: The Crossroad Publishing Company 1987), pp. 24–26.

when we hear the word "kingdom," we tend to think of the territory over which God rules rather than God's rule itself. In the *Quest of the Historic Jesus*, Albert Schweitzer[25] called attention to a study by Gustaf Dalman, who maintained that behind the Greek term basileia (kingdom) stands an Aramaic term which actually means a king's rule or reign and not the territory over which he rules.[26] Norman Perrin accepted the views of Schweitzer and Dalman on this point and traced the history of the term in his book, *The Kingdom of God in the Teaching of Jesus*.[27] In other words Mark wrote about the coming of God's rule, and described Jesus as the one to whom God delegate divine authority. When Mark wrote that Jesus, " . . . taught them as one having authority, and not as the scribes," he meant divine and not human authority (Mk. 1:22).

Although Mark participated in the apocalyptic worldview, the gospel is not an apocalypse like the Book of Revelation.[28] A good model for understanding Mark's relation to apocalyptic is that of Greg Carey, who used the terms apocalyptic discourse and apocalyptic topics and suggested the following "definition,"

> Thus, apocalyptic discourse should be treated as a flexible set of resources that early Jews and Christians could employ for a variety of persuasive tasks.[29]

The notion of apocalyptic discourse enables us to bring together a number of topics from different genres and equate them. For example, the combat myth in Genesis[30] becomes the tribulation

25. Albert Schweitzer, *The Quest of the Historical Jesus*, translated by W. Montgomery, (Great Britain: A&C Black Ltd. 1910), p. 270.

26. Gustaf Dalman, *The Words of Jesus*, p. 94.

27. Norman Perrin, *The Kingdom of God in the Teachings of Jesus*, (London: SCM Press Ltd, 1963), pp. 23, 28.

28. John J. Collins, *The Apocalyptic Imagination*, p. 4. He defines an apocalypse as: "a genre of revelatory literature with a narrative framework, in which a revelation is mediated by an otherworldly being to a human recipient, disclosing a transcendent reality which is both temporal, insofar as it envisages eschatological salvation, and spatial insofar as it involved another supernatural world."

29. Greg Carey, *Ultimate Things*, (St. Louis, Missouri: Chalice Press, 2005), p. 5 and 12.

30. The reflection of the Babylonian Combat myth in the creation story is

in Mark (Mk. 13:19), and the combat myth in revelation (Rev. 12, 19:11–21).[31] And the rule of God in Genesis becomes the Kingdom (rule) of God in Mark, and the Kingdom of God in the book of Revelation.

> The kingdom of the world has become the kingdom of our Lord and his Messiah (Rev. 11:15).

Finally, with the complete "defeat" of the destructive waters of creation in Revelation God's rule is described as a new creation.

> Then I saw a new heaven and a new earth for the first heaven and the first earth had passed away, and *the sea was no more* (Rev. 21:1).

The creation represented order and the sea chaos, and to say "the sea was no more" was to say that chaos was defeated and the kingdom of God was established.

The Debates: Jesus as a Child Prodigy Debater

While Mark dealt only with Jesus as an adult debater, according to Luke Jesus honed his debating skills early on (Lk. 41–46). After attending the festival of Passover, Jesus' parents returned home with a group of friends and relatives. Jesus, who was twelve-years-old, stayed behind in Jerusalem. Through a faulty headcount Jesus' parents—like many since—did not notice his absence. After searching among their entourage to no avail, they went back to Jerusalem only to find him in the Temple sitting, among the teachers engaging in a friendly debate or discussion. Luke says the teachers were "amazed

---

brought out clearly in Theophile J. Meeks translation of Genesis 1:1-2 in *The Bible An American Translation, The Old Testament*, Editor J. M. Powis Smith, (Chicago, Illinois, The University of Chicago Press, 1939), p. 1. "When God began to create the heavens and the earth, the earth was a desolate waste, with darkness covering the abyss and a tempestuous wind raging over the surface of the waters."

31. Adela Yarbro Collins, *The Combat Myth in the Book of Revelation*, (Eugene, OR: Wipf and Stock Publishers, 2001), pp. 57–100. Previously published by Harvard Theological Review, 1976. See Rev. 12 and 19:11–21.

at his understanding and his answers" (Lk. 2:47). While Luke attributed a favorable response to Jesus' debating skills to the teachers in the Temple, Mark attributed a similar favorable response to Jesus' debate performances to the crowds (Mk. 12:37). In Mark the Temple authorities remained Jesus' implacable enemies to the end.

Perhaps a word is in order about the probable origin of such an unlikely story. Very great men are sometimes presumed to have had an equally remarkable childhood. It was unthinkable that such greatness did not manifest itself even in childhood. In this respect Luke's story resembles that of the Apocryphal Infancy Gospels.[32] While in Luke in was a matter of intellectual prowess, in the apocryphal gospels it was often a case of the boy Jesus exhibiting great feats of magical powers sometimes used for mischievous purposes.

James M. Robinson: The Apocalyptic Struggle and the Debates in Mark

As the title of Robinson's book, *The Problem of History in Mark*, shows, his primary interest was in Mark's view of history, which he took to consist of an apocalyptic struggle between God and Satan. According to Robinson this conflict is revealed explicitly in Jesus' exorcism and implicitly in his debates with his opponents, and even in the disputes with his own disciples. Robinson's main contribution to the understanding of the debates resides in the connection he drew between the exorcisms and the debates, demonstrating a formal similarity between them.[33] This connection proved that the debates were not intended to result in a consensus or compromise, but rather total victory of good over evil, God over Satan. From the exorcisms to the debates only the means varied not the aim of the contest. One is reminded of what Carl von Clausewitz said of war being the continuation of politics by other means.

---

32. Edgar Hennecke, *New Testament Apocrypha*, ed. Wilhelm Schneemelcher, (Philadelphia: The Westminster Press, 1959), *The Infancy of Thomas*, pp. 388–401.

33. James M. Robinson, *The Problem of History in Mark and Other Marcan Studies*, (Philadelphia: Fortress Press, 1982), p. 92.

However, by denying the importance of Jesus use of logic in Mark Robinson overlooked the value Mark attached to the battle of wits in the debates.[34] This oversight is in turn connected with Robinson's reliance on Form Critical categories and denial that the debates had a single form.[35] Rhetorical studies have since shown that the major debates in Mark did adhere to a single form, the enthymeme.[36] Although Robinson mentioned three of the main debates about divorce, paying taxes to Caesar, and the Beelzebub debate,[37] he did not discuss them in detail. The closest he came to describing the course of a debate was in his account of the Beelzebub debate,[38] which was the one that best illustrated Mark's view of history as an apocalyptic struggle. While Robinson did not discuss the course of the debates, his work remains the best description of their Cosmic context. In fact Robinson considered the parable of the strong man, which follows the Beelzebub debate, the key to the Gospel of Mark (Mk. 3:20–27).[39]

Jesus as a Mature Debater[40]

With this cosmic background in mind we will now turn to a consideration of the rhetorical argumentative forms these debates

---

34. Ibid., p. 98.

35. Ibid., p. 92.

36. Mary Ann Tolbert, *Sowing the Gospel*, (Minneapolis: Fortress Press, 1989), pp. 250ff.

37. James M. Robinson, *The Problem of History in Mark and Other Marcan Studies*, p. 96–98.

38. Ibid., p. 84.

39. Ibid., p. 79.

40. Joanna Dewey, *Markan Public Debate, Literary Technique, Concentric Structure and Theology in Mar 2:1—3:6*, (Chico, CA: Scholars Press, 1980), passim. Although she entitled her book *Markan Public Debate*, her subtitle reflected her primary interest, which is in the literary structure of Mark, a perfectly legitimate enterprise. But one looks in vain in her book for a discussion of the course of the debates themselves. Her book fulfills the promise of the subtitle, but not the title. James Robinson had already used the terms "public debate" in his book *The Problem of History in Mark and Other Marcan Studies*, p. 91.

COMPLEX RHETORICAL ARGUMENTS

between Jesus and his opponents took. While the "gar" (for) enthymemes are largely confined to the comments by the author of the gospel, the more complex arguments are described in the context of controversies between Jesus and his opponents. Even though the enthymemes (arguments) remain basically the same in nature, in the give and take of an extended debate they tend to become more complex and the necessity to reconstruct their underlying syllogistic form more urgent. The best reconstruction of these complex rhetorical syllogisms is found in Mary Ann Tolbert's book *Sowing the Gospel*.

According to Tolbert:

> Though the content of Jesus' controversies and teachings mostly deal with Jewish belief and practice, the form of his argument is thoroughly Hellenistic.[41]

Like Kennedy, she defined the enthymeme as an "abbreviated syllogism," which "may occur simply as a statement with an accompanying reason."[42] However, behind this simple form stood a complete syllogism, which Mark's audience, since it shared the speaker's premises, could easily reconstruct. But what was clear to the ancient audience may not be as clear to the modern audience, so Tolbert reconstructed the syllogism underlying three of Mark's complex enthymemes: the one about the advisability of paying taxes to Caesar, another about the resurrection, and finally one about whose son the Messiah is.

To these I will add two more lengthy arguments about the permissibility of divorce (Mk. 10:2–12), in which Jesus used the word arché with the probable meaning "first principle," which I discussed in Appendix II of my book, *Mark: A Twice-Told Tale*,[43] and the Beelzebub debate.

---

41. Mary Ann Tolbert, *Sowing the Gospel*, pp. 250–256.
42. *Ibid.*, p. 250.
43. Caurie Beaver, *Mark: A Twice-Told Tale*, pp. 234–237. The argument about whose son the Messiah is appeared as Appendix I.

The Argument about Paying Taxes to Caesar

The first complex enthymeme discussed by Tolbert was the one about paying taxes to Caesar. This debate was part of an ongoing conflict with the authorities, which began with Jesus' cleansing of the Temple. The Temple authorities questioned Jesus' right to do what he did; they asked "by what authority are you doing these things?" (Mk. 11:28) Jesus responded by asking them about the source of John the Baptist's authority, which the Jerusalem leaders had not accepted, but could not openly challenge due to his popularity with the people, who considered him a prophet. Then Jesus told the Parable of the Vineyard, which pointed to the imminent destruction of the whole tax gathering system. The Temple authorities wanted to arrest Jesus but feared the people and left him instead.

"Then *they* sent to Jesus some Pharisees and Herodians to trap him in what he said" (Mk. 12:13). The "they" in this quotation leads through a series of pronouns back to the antecedent "the chief priests, scribes, and elders" who had challenged Jesus' authority earlier in the Temple (Mk. 11:27). "They" are represented in the present passage as deputizing and sending "some Pharisees" and "some Herodians," who, after an obsequiously flattering introduction, spring a trap for Jesus by asking a trick question:

> Teacher, we know that you are sincere and show deference to no one; for you do not regard people with partiality, but teach the way of God in accordance with truth. Is it lawful to pay taxes to the emperor or not? Should we pay them or should we not? (Mk. 12:14–15)

Since taxes were unpopular, if Jesus said, "Yes," the people would have deserted him, and if he said, "No," the Romans would have arrested him. Jesus, "knowing their hypocrisy, said to them, 'Why are you putting me to the test?'" (Mk. 12:15). So with Solomon-like wisdom he turned the tables on his questioners by asking for a Roman coin, and asking whose image was on it. They answered, "The emperor's." Then Jesus answered their original question by saying, "Give to the emperor the things that are the emperor's and to God the things that are God's" (Mk. 12:13–17). Tolbert's reconstruction of the syllogism behind Jesus' argument is brilliant and deserves to be quoted in full here. She wrote:

> Jesus responds by enunciating two enthymemes, one overt and one implied, derived from the same suppressed major premise:

Major premise:	
Whatever bears the image and inscription of someone belongs to that one	
Overt minor premise:	Implied minor premise:
a denarius carries Caesar's image and words (Mk. 12:16)	Human beings are in the image of God (see Gen. 1:26–28).
Conclusion:	Conclusion:
'Render to Caesar the things that are Caesar's' (Mk. 12:17)	'and to God the things that are God's' (Mk. 12:17)

Mark says, "And they were utterly amazed at him" (Mk. 12:17b).[44]

The Argument about the Resurrection

Tolbert's second reconstructed enthymeme was about the belief in the resurrection. The argument was between the Sadducees, who did not believe in the resurrection, and Jesus, who did. In the debate that followed Tolbert said that the Sadducees used a rhetorical example, which is less convincing and Jesus used an enthymeme, which is more persuasive. It should also be noted that the Sadducees based their reasoning on the Torah because they were "strict constructionists" and rejected the later interpretations of it. Their argument against the resurrection involved a reductio ad absurdum argument resulting from their hypothetical projection of marriage into the afterlife. They cited the cases of levirate marriage (Gen. 38:8–11, Deut. 25:5–10):

---

44. Mary Ann Tolbert, *Sowing the Gospel*, p. 251.

> Teacher, Moses wrote for us that if a man's brother dies, leaving a wife but no child, the man shall marry the widow and raise up children for his brother.

Then they told a story of seven brothers who married a woman one after the other, and died leaving no children. Finally, the woman also died. The Sadducees asked, "In the resurrection whose wife will she be?" Apparently, the Sadducees did not tolerate polyandry or she could have been the wife of all seven brothers in the resurrection.

Jesus' opening argument that in the resurrection there would be no marriage because we would be like the angels probably carried little weight with the Sadducees because they did not believe in angels. However, he based his main argument for the resurrection on a passage from the Torah, which the Sadducees did accept. They quoted Moses, so Jesus quoted Moses:

> And as for the dead being raised have you not read in the book of Moses, in the story about the bush, how God said to him, "I am the God of Abraham, the God of Isaac, and the God of Jacob?" he is the God not of the dead, but of the living," (Mk. 12:26–27).

My reconstruction of the full syllogism underlying Jesus enthymeme (argument) differs slightly from Tolbert's.

> Major Premise: God is not the God of the dead but of the living.
> Minor Premise: God is the God Abraham, Isaac, and Jacob.
> Conclusion: Therefore, Abraham, Isaac, and Jacob are living.

Oddly enough Jesus' argument does not prove a universal resurrection because if God is not your God, you would remain dead.

The Argument about Whose Son the Messiah Is

The third complex enthymeme, the underlying syllogism of which Tolbert reconstructed, is the one about whose son the Messiah is. Since I disagree with her conclusion in regard to this argument, it will require an extended treatment, which I have already given it in

Appendix I of my book *Mark: A Twice-Told Tale*. Therefore, I have decided to include the entire Appendix I here.[45]

The Messiah: God's Son Not David's

Since the Messiah is now generally regarded as the Son of David by both Jews and Christians, it is surprising that Mark does not share this common opinion. It was frequently asserted that Mark retained the notion of the Davidic descent of the Messiah and the title Son of David for Jesus purged of its nationalistic associations, and elevated to a higher level.

It will be the contention of this appendix that Mark rejected the title Son of David altogether and had Jesus claim that the Messiah was God's son not David's.

> While Jesus was teaching in the temple, he said, "How can the scribes say that the Messiah is the son of David? David himself, by the Holy Spirit declared, 'the Lord said to my Lord, "Sit at my right hand, until I put your enemies under your feet."' David himself calls him Lord; so how can he be his son?" and the large crowd was listening to him with delight. (RSV Mk. 12:35-37).

The traditional belief that Jesus was a descendent of David, has led to a distorted and contradictory pattern of commentary on this passage: The commentator first acknowledges the straight forward meaning of these verses, refers to the traditional view, and then rejects the obvious explanation in favor of the traditional one.

Anticipating his rejection of the obvious meaning of the passage, Branscomb asserted, "This is a strange and difficult passage."[46] Following the above pattern he first acknowledged its plain meaning.

---

45. Caurie Beaver, *Mark: A Twice-Told Tale*, pp. 209-216.
46. Harvie Branscomb, *The Gospel of Mark, The Moffat New Testament Commentary*, (London: Hadder Stoughton Limited, 1952), p. 222.

"Jesus attacks the teaching of the scribes that the Christ is David's son, and affirms instead that he is David's Lord."[47]

Then he referred to the traditional belief as to Jesus' descent.

But what is denied is exactly what Christians from Paul's day on believed-namely that Jesus was a descendant of David (see Rom. 1:3, and the genealogies in Matt. and Luke).[48]

Finally, he rejected the obvious meaning of the passage.

"By the time he (Mark) wrote, belief in the Davidic lineage of Jesus was no doubt current throughout the Christian movement. Mark certainly did not doubt it."[49]

A more recent commentator, Hugh Anderson, followed the same pattern. First he acknowledged the plain sense of the passage.

"If the saying, of verse 35b-37 is authentic, it is most natural to suppose that in debate with his opponents Jesus was defending the (non-Davidic) character of his Messiahship against the popular Jewish recognition that Messiah must be of David's line."[50]

Then he also referred to the traditional view.

" ... the early church... universally accepted the Davidic descent of Jesus ... and had apparently no objection to 'Son of David' as a title for Jesus (Mt. 1:6, Lk. 2:4; 3:31; Rom. 1:3; 2 Tim. 2:8).[51]

Anderson then rejected the plain meaning of the passage asserting that, " ... the Hellenistic church saw in it the evidence that Jesus was not just Son of David but Son of God (cf. 15:39) ."[52]

47. Ibid., p. 222.
48. Ibid., p. 222.
49. Ibid., p. 222.
50. Hugh Anderson, *The Gospel of Mark*, New Century Bible Commentary, (Grand Rapids: Wm .B. Eerdmans Pub. Co., 1976) pp. 284.
51. Ibid., p. 284.
52. Ibid., p. 284.

Anderson raised two issues, which should be distinguished: the Davidic descent of the Messiah and "Son of David" as a title for the Messiah. Two other issues also need to be distinguished: the Davidic descent of the Messiah and the Davidic descent of Jesus. The designation, "Son of David" appears to have originated with Mark-in the New Testament at least-and was passed on to Matthew and Luke. It also appears to be limited to the synoptic gospels (Mk. 10:47, 10:48, and 12:35; Mt. 1:1, 1:20, 12:23, 15:22, 20:30, 20:31, 21:9, 21:15, 22:42; Lk. 3:31, 18:38, and 18:39).

The strongest affirmation of the Davidic descent of the Messiah is found in Schweizer's commentary on Mark. After conceding that " . . . the easiest interpretation of the statement." is, " . . . that he (Jesus) is disputing the Davidic descent of the Messiah."[53] Schweizer goes on to claim,

> "The Davidic descent of the Messiah, however, is not denied in the Christian writings prior to the Epistle of Barnabas (12:10f.), and there it occurred as the result of an anti-Jewish attitude. Otherwise Jesus is regarded universally as David's descendant."[54]

What Schweizer failed to say was how seldom the Davidic descent of the Messiah was affirmed. A glance at a concordance will reveal how infrequently David is even mentioned in the New Testament at least in only nine of the 27 books. Therefore, it does not appear to be true that Jesus was universally acknowledged as David's descendant. If Mark denied the Davidic descent of Jesus, then Schweizer's other claim that Barnabas was the first to deny it would also be inaccurate.

Finally, we come to an author who at first seems to appreciate the full force of Mark's argument. Tolbert's is by far the best and most complete analysis of Mark's /Jesus' reasoning. She claims rightly that this saying is cast in the form of an enthymeme or rhetorical syllogism (a truncated form of argument ordinarily used in

---

53. Edward Schweizer, *The Good News According to Mark*, (Richmond, Virginia: John Knox Press, 1970), p. 256.

54. Ibid., p. 256.

public speaking) in which the major premise was omitted. Because the premise was a belief shared by the audience and speaker, it was simply left unstated. Syllogisms and enthymemes differ in at least two respects. First the syllogism is more complete exhibiting the major premise, minor premise and conclusion. Second, it utilizes as premises notions that are universally agreed upon.

> Major premise: All men are mortal
> Minor premise: Socrates is a man.
> Conclusion: Socrates is mortal.

Enthymemes substitute for these universal propositions common opinions, folk wisdom, or probable truths that are more likely to be culturally and historically conditioned. Therefore, the conclusions drawn are only probable. For example, an enthymeme/syllogism can be formed from the proverbial saying, "Spare the rod and spoil the child" (Prov. 13:24).

> Major premise: Parents who do not use the rod to discipline their children spoil them.
> Minor premise: Mrs. Jones did not use the rod on her children.
> Conclusion: Mrs. Jones spoiled her children.

The rod was a rather harsh instrument of discipline, the use of which we would probably consider child abuse now. Paul said he was beaten with rods three times (2 Cor. 11:25). The enthymeme/syllogism we would form from such information would be quite different.

> Major premise: Parents who use the rod to discipline their children abuse them by teaching them to solve problems by resorting to violence.
> Minor premise: Mrs. Jones used the rod to correct her children.
> Conclusion: Mrs. Jones abused her children.

Unlike Jesus' / Mark's audience, the gospel's modern readers may not find the premises, whether expressed or unexpressed, so obvious, the Davidic authorship of Psalm 110, for example. Therefore, Tolbert was right to reconstruct the full syllogism or complete logical form of the argument underlying the enthymeme. According to Tolbert,

> . . . Jesus interprets an accepted messianic text enthymematically. He begins by stating the view of the scribes, which he intends to refute, 'that the Christ is the son of David' (12:35) and then constructs his scriptural enthymeme with a suppressed major premise draw from customary mores:

Suppressed major premise: Fathers do not address their sons with titles of respect like "sir" or "master."
Minor premise: David declared "The Lord said to my master, 'Sit at my right hand, till I put your enemies under your feet'" (Mk. 12:36).
Conclusion: The one David calls master cannot be his son.

> Because fathers do not call their sons master, David's reference to the Christ as my master (or "my lord") proves that the Christ cannot be David's son in any traditional sense. It is possible to understand Jesus as "Son of David" only if one recognizes that title as describing one aspect of Jesus' broader role as heir of the vineyard.[55]

To this conclusion that the messiah cannot be David's son Tolbert adds a number of qualifications. The messiah cannot be David's son "in any traditional sense," unless it is combined with Jesus' broader role as "heir of the vineyard," and with no "literal attempt to trace Davidic lineage as a test of messiahship." None of these qualifications are found in Mark. She is right when she writes, "The Christ is God's heir, not David's."[56] However, this accurate statement has to be contrasted with an opposite affirmation made by her elsewhere.

> Chapter 10: Jesus the Heir of the Vineyard will discuss the parable of the Tenants and the dominant portrayal

---

55. Mary Ann Tolbert, *Sowing the Gospel*, pp. 255–256.
56. Ibid., p. 256.

Mark's Argumentative Jesus

of Jesus in Division Two as the true heir, the Son of David, the authoritative interpreter of Jewish Scripture and tradition.[57]

Like other commentators Tolbert, after acknowledging the plain meaning of the passage, proceeded to reject it.

Tolbert performed identical operations on two previous enthymemes in Mark: the one about paying taxes to Caesar (Mk. 12:13–17),[58] and the one about the resurrection (Mk. 12:18–27).[59] In these two instances she simply accepted Mark's conclusions without qualification, apparently because she found nothing controversial in them.

The most consistent interpretation of this passage is that of Werner Kelber. He claimed that Mark rejected the Davidic descent of the messiah, and pointed out that Mark also rejected Bartimaeus' hailing of Jesus as the Son of David by representing him as blind when he uttered the confession. Finally, when Jesus entered Jerusalem, the crowd shouted, "Blessed is the coming Kingdom of our father David" (Mk. 11:10). Kelber contrasted the kingdom of their father David with the kingdom of Jesus' father God.[60]

However, it is Tolbert's concept of Jesus as the heir of the vineyard that explains why Mark rejected the Davidic descent of the messiah. To say that Jesus as God's son inherited the vineyard was to say that the Jewish leaders as David's sons did not. They were simply tenants of the vineyard. When the tenants killed the beloved son, the vineyard passed not to them, but to Jesus' family the ones who did the will of God-the Markan community!

These authors, except for Kelber, rejected Mark's conclusion in regard to the Messiah's lineage because they viewed the gospel through the set of beliefs shaped by Formative Rabbinical Judaism and Matthean Sectarian Judaism. There is no doubt about the prevalence of the belief in the Davidic descent of the Messiah

57. Ibid., p. 126.
58. Ibid., p. 251.
59. Ibid., p. 252.
60. Werner Kelber, *The Kingdom in Mark*, (Philadelphia: Fortress Press, 1974), pp. 95–97.

among the scribes (of the Pharisees) and Paul, who was also a Pharisee. Apparently Matthew agreed with Formative Judaism against Mark on this point. In fact Matthew's most drastic revision of Mark was to add a genealogy to Mark's narrative showing Jesus' descent from David.

However, Mark represented the period preceding the war between Rome and Judea in which a number of alternative messianic notions still existed. The Essenes at Qumran, for example, expected a messiah or messiahs of Aaron and Israel.[61] To understand how these various messianic notions arose one must go back to the history and stream(s) of tradition, what Greg Riley called the River of God. The Davidic dynasty came to an end in the Exile, which for some groups weakened the connection between the house of David and the Messianic hope.

With the return from the Exile, the rebuilding of the temple, and the concentration on the Torah, priest and scribes came to fill the power vacuum. The returning community was led by Ezra, a scribe not a royal prince. It was a family of priests who sparked the Maccabean revolt, and the subsequent power struggles revolved around priests not kings. That explains how the Essenes came to expect a messiah of Aaron and the book of Hebrews called Jesus a High Priest (Heb. 4:14—5:14) as well as the Son of God. Though Hebrews mentioned the tribe of Judah, it has nothing about the Davidic descent of Jesus. Like Mark, Hebrews preferred the title Son of God and did not mention the title Son of David. The author went so far as to specifically reject genealogies (Matthew/Luke) in favor of Jesus' priesthood being like that of Melchizedek, who had neither father nor mother (Heb. 7:3). Like Mark, Hebrews emphasized that Jesus as the son of God was heir as opposed to Moses, who was a servant (Heb. 3:5–6).

In addition to this indigenous priestly role for the messiah there were other models suggested by the surrounding cultures. Mark called the Messiah the Son of Man and the Son of God, which probably reflected Persian and Hellenistic conceptions.

---

61. James C. Vanderkam, *The Dead Sea Scrolls Today*, (Grand Rapids, Michigan: William B. Eerdmans Publishing Company, 1994), p. 177.

Zoroastrian eschatology tended to emphasize divine Saviors, like the Son of Man in Daniel and Mark, instead of earthly deliverers like David. Similarly, Hellenistic religion tended to elevate great earthly leaders, like Alexander the Great and some Roman Caesars to divine status. Since Mark's eschatology, like Persian eschatology, led him to emphasize the messiah's divine connections, it is not surprising that he rejected the notion that the messiah was the Son of David.

The Argument about Divorce: The Guiding Principle (arché) of Creation[62]

It is worthwhile to ask whether Mark used the term arché elsewhere in the gospel in the logical sense. He used arché three other times: Mk. 10: 6, and 13: 8 and 9. In the last two references the temporal element may predominate: The second arché (Mk. 13: 8) referred to the beginning of the tribulation period, a time of wars like Armageddon that preceded the end of the world, and the third one (Mk. 13: 9) to the time since the beginning of creation.

However, in the first reference (Mk. 10: 6) the context would suggest that a non-temporal or logical meaning was primarily intended. In a complex argument about divorce Mark had Jesus appeal to God's creation as the basis of his reasoning. The poetic version in Genesis is frequently used in the marriage ceremony, but Mark's Jesus used it in a reasoned argument about the permissibility of divorce. The Pharisees had just challenged Jesus with the question as to whether it was lawful for a man to put away (divorce) his wife. Jesus in turn asked them what Moses *commanded*. They replied that Moses *permitted* divorce by a bill of divorcement. Jesus then argued that Moses allowed divorce because of the hardness of their hearts, but maintained that the original intention of creation was otherwise.

---

62. Caurie Beaver, *Mark: A Twice-Told Tale*, Appendix II, pp. 234–237.

In order to follow Jesus' reasoning one must have both creation stories in mind. We will list them in the Genesis order although the first one is probably later than the second one.

The First Creation Story

> So God created humankind in his image
> in the image of God he created them;
> male and female he created them. (Gen. 1: 27)

The Second Creation Story

—then the Lord God formed man from the dust of the ground, and breathed into his nostrils the breath of life; and the man became a living being. (Gen. 2: 7).

So the Lord God caused a deep sleep to fall upon the man, and he slept; then he took one of his ribs and closed up its place with flesh. And the rib that the Lord God had taken from the man He made into a woman and brought her to the man.

> Then the man said,
> 'This at last is bone of my bones
> and flesh of my flesh;
> This one shall be called woman,
> For out of man this one was taken.'
> Therefore (Mark has 'for this reason')
> a man leaves his father and his
> mother and clings to his wife,
> and they become one
> flesh. (Gen. 2: 21–23)

After pointing out that Moses' bill of divorcement was a concession to man's weakness, Jesus continued,

Mark / Jesus' Creation Story

> But from the beginning (arché) of creation, 'God made them male and female.' (from the first creation story, Gen. 1: 27).
>
> For this reason a man shall leave his father and mother and be joined to his wife, and the two shall become one flesh. So they are no longer two, but one flesh. (from the second creation story, Gen. 2: 24–25).
>
> Therefore what God has joined together, let no one separate. (Mk. 10: 6–9)

Jesus' argument required the use of both creation stories. In the gospel of Mark Jesus maintained that divorce was forbidden because God joined male and female together, which required that they be created separately in the first place as in the first creation story. Just the opposite happened in the second creation story in which male and female were originally together in Adam, and God separated them by taking Adam's rib and creating woman. In the second creation story it was unnecessary for God to join man and woman together. The man simply leaves his parents and clings to his wife, and they become one flesh because they were originally created as one. The phrase "For this reason" makes more sense in the second creation story in which the rationale for a man's leaving his father and mother and clinging to his wife is that the man and woman were created together in the first place. When Mark / Jesus made this phrase follow the first creation story in which God created male and female separately at the beginning, it loses some of its force.

Mark / Jesus required the separate creation of man and woman, because his argument required that God join them together. His reasoning can be cast in the form of a syllogism.

> Major Premise: What God joined together man must not separate.
> Minor Premise: God joined man and wife together as one flesh.

Conclusion: Therefore, no man shall separate them.

The Beelzebub Debate

After Jesus had appointed the twelve disciples, he returned home and the crowds gathered,

> so that they could not even eat. When his family heard it, they went out to restrain him, for the people were saying, "He has gone out of his mind," and the scribes who came down from Jerusalem said, "He has Beelzebub, and by the ruler of the demons he casts out demons" (Mk. 3:19b-22).

The people's accusation that Jesus had lost his mind already introduced the notion that he was demon possessed, because the people believed that mental illness was caused by demons (Mk. 3:21). Therefore, when the scribes, who came down from Jerusalem, said, "He has Beelzebub" (Mk. 3:22), they were saying essentially the same thing as the people, with the addition that he was possessed by not just any demon, but by the ruler of the demons. This is an example of what Elaine Pagels described as the tendency to demonize one's opponent, which has a long and notorious history, both within and outside Christianity.[63]

This "charge" provoked Jesus to tell the Parable of Satan's Divided Kingdom, and the Binding of the Strong Man:

> How can Satan cast out Satan? If a kingdom is divided against itself, that kingdom cannot stand; and if a house if divided against itself, that house will not be able to stand. And if Satan has risen up against himself and is divided, he cannot stand, but his end has come. But no one can enter a strong man's house and plunder his property without first tying up that strong man; then indeed the house can be plundered (Mk. 3:23–27).

---

63. Elaine Pagels, *The Origin of Satan*, (New York: First Vintage Books Edition, 1996), passim.

This parable begins with a rhetorical question very similar to the one that introduced the argument about whose son the Messiah is, "How can the scribes say that the Messiah is the son of David?" (Mk. 12:35). Both questions are followed by transparent rhetorical syllogisms:

1. The Rhetorical Question: How Can Satan Cast Out Satan? (Mk. 3:23b)
2. Major Premise: A Kingdom or house that is divided against itself cannot stand (Mk. 3:24, 25).
3. Minor premise: Assuming that (if) Satan has risen up against himself and is divided (Mk. 3:26a).
4. Conclusion: Satan cannot stand, but "has an end."

This is obviously a hypothetical syllogism, for if Satan were helping Jesus by casting out his own horde of demons, there would be no need for Jesus to bind him before entering his house because in that case Satan "has an end" (Mk. 3:26).

Joel Marcus translated this key phrase "has an end" as "was coming to an end." This prepared for Marcus' shift from considering the parable countrafactual or hypothetical to a factual one describing "the way things actually are." In Marcus' own words:

> Jesus begins by arguing contrafactually: if he were casting out demons by Satan, that would mean that Satan had risen against himself, that his dominion and household were divided, that his reign "was coming to an end."[64]

When Marcus twisted the hypothetical parable of the Divided Dominion so that it became a factual parable representing things the way they were, he completely missed the point of the parable. He added the Parable of the binding of the Strong Man (Satan) to the hypothetical parable about Satan casting out Satan and concluded that Jesus bound the Strong Man and was plundering his divided kingdom so that it *"was coming* to an end," and not *"has* an end." Then he concluded, "The situation presented by the parable of the

---

64. Joel Marcus, *Mark 1–8*, pp. 281–282.

Divided dominion and House, then, is *not* contrafactual but a portrayal of the way things actually are."[65]

However, the hypothetical parable did not say that Satan's kingdom "was coming to an end," but "has an end," in which case there would have been no need to bind the Strong Man. Furthermore, there is no warrant in the text whatsoever to shift from a contrafactual (hypothetical) view of the Divided Kingdom Parable. It makes perfect sense as it is. The conclusion of the hypothetical syllogism is that Satan by casting out Satan is divided and has an end. But since the syllogism is hypothetical, the real implication of Mark's or Jesus' argument is that Satan is not divided but united and very strong. That is why in the very next parable he is called the Strong Man, and why it is still necessary for Jesus, the one who is stronger than John the Baptist (Mk. 1:7), to bind him before plundering his house. Satan's kingdom is not coming to an end by internal division and uprisings but by Jesus' exorcism activity.

If the scribes can be provocative in accusing Jesus of casting out Satan with the help of the ruler of demons, Jesus can be equally threatening in his counter thrust.

> Truly I tell you, people will be forgiven for their sins and whatever blasphemies they utter; but whoever blasphemes against the Holy Spirit can never have forgiveness, but is guilty of an eternal sin—for they said, "He has an unclean spirit" (Mk. 3:28-30).

The only equally uncompromising denial of forgiveness in the New Testament is found in the book of Hebrews (Heb. 6:4-6).

This cosmic background of the debates broke through once again in the conflict between Jesus and Peter over Jesus' prediction of his imminent death and resurrection in Jerusalem:

> Then he began to teach them that the Son of Man must undergo great suffering, and be rejected by the elders, the chief priests and scribes, and be killed, and after three days rise again. He said all this quite openly. And Peter took him aside and began to rebuke him. But turning

---

65. Ibid., p. 282.

and looking at his disciples, he rebuked Peter and said, "Get behind me Satan! For you are setting your mind not on a divine things but on human things" (Mk. 8:31-33).

The first thing to notice about Jesus' "prediction" is that Mark did not quote Jesus as he did in the second and third predictions of the passion (Mk. 9:31, 32; 10:33, 34). In the first predictions of Jesus' death and resurrection Mark is speaking and not Jesus, so the reference to the Son of Man in the third person is natural here. the second thing to notice is that Peter's rebuke has no content; we are not told why he objected to Jesus' death. However, we know from the disciples' failure to understand about the loaves (Mk. 6:52) that they did not understand the broken bread as the broken body of the Son of Man. When Jesus broke the bread at the Last Supper, as he had done before when he fed the multitudes, perhaps the disciples began to understand. The parabolic references to Jesus' death as broken bread only brought about incomprehension on the part of the disciples, but when Jesus spoke plainly about his death, Peter objected.

Finally, whatever Peter said in his rebuke did not please Jesus, as his rebuke of Peter shows. When Jesus said to Peter, "Get behind me, Satan!" (Mk. 8:3), some commentators say that Jesus was telling Peter literally to "go away after me" as he did when he first call him, "come after me" (Mk. 1:17).[66] In other words, "Get back in line" or "Get back to following me," and, "if any want to become my followers, let them deny themselves and take up their cross and follow me" (Mk. 8:34). In this passage, Mark spelled out where Jesus was asking Peter to follow him to, namely, where he was going, to his death in Jerusalem.

Elizabeth E. Shively: Mark as Apocalyptic Narrative

Shively, like Robinson, chose the Beelzebub debate as the key to the Gospel of Mark: Robinson chose it to illustrate Mark's

---

66. C. Clifton Black, *Mark, Abingdon New Testament Commentaries*, (Nashville: Abingdon Press, 2011), p. 195. He relates the expression to the theme of following Jesus.

apocalyptic view of history and Shively selected it to show that Mark is an apocalyptic narrative. While Robinson highlighted the binding of the strong man, Satan (Mk. 3:27), Shively began with an exhaustive study of the entire passage in question (Mk. 3:22–30). Robinson's book is the best treatment of Mark's view of history as a cosmic apocalyptic struggle; Shively's work is an unparalleled revelation of the extent to which apocalyptic thought determined the literary structure of Mark. However, in my view the rhetorical approach reveals the course of the debated better than either the historical or literary approaches.

Shively agreed with Robinson—against Joel Marcus—that Satan remained strong throughout Jesus' ministry, and by no means ruled a house divided as the scribes' accusation implied.[67] Otherwise it would not have been necessary for Jesus to bind him before entering his dwelling. Shively's use of Greg Carey's notions of apocalyptic discourse and apocalyptic topics to reveal the programmatic character of this debate in the plot of Mark's story is nothing less than brilliant.[68]

However, I cannot accept her characterization of Mark's genre as apocalyptic narrative.[69] Of course, Mark is an apocalyptic narrative, but narrative is not a genre but a characteristic of a number of genres. In my opinion, Mark is a persuasive discourse or speech. Again Shively's literary approach is perfectly legitimate for analyzing Mark's story, but in my view the persuasive elements in the gospel are dominant and require a rhetorical approach. However, it must not be forgotten that a story is an argument in narrative form and an argument is a story in discursive form.

---

67. Elizabeth E. Shively, *Apocalyptic Imagination in the Gospel of Mark: The Literary and Theological Role of Mark 3:22–30*, (Go[set umlaut over o]ttingen, Germany, Walter de Gruyter & Co. KB, Berlin and Boston, 2012), p. 257.

68. Ibid., p. 256.

69. Ibid., p. 252.

Chapter VI

The Enthymeme or Rhetorical Syllogism that Generated Mark's Persuasive Speech

Mark's Structural Enthymeme

THUS FAR, MARK HAS portrayed Jesus as engaging in debates with various opponents. The chief priests, scribes, and the elders questioned Jesus' authority to "cleanse" the temple; the Pharisees and Herodians tried to trap him with a question about paying taxes to Caesar; and the Sadducees attempted to stump him with a riddle about the resurrection. In each case, Jesus argued one side of the question, and his opponents argued the other. Mark represented the parties to these debates as Jesus' opponents.

However, when Mark made an argument of his own, we have to ask who *his* opponents were. When Jesus began to teach the three disciples, Peter, James, and John, about the resurrection of the Son of Man on the mountain, they raised an objection of Jesus' opponents—the scribes—that Elijah must come first. But Mark, himself, had already begun to teach essentially the same thing as Jesus did on the mountain by calling his message the gospel of Jesus Christ, and by quoting the prophecy of "Isaiah" in which God promised to send the messenger (Elijah) before the Lord (Mk 1:1–3). However, literary critics point out that only the reader knew

The Enthymeme or Rhetorical Syllogism

what Mark wrote, so Jesus had to repeat it for the disciples on the mountain. Jesus told the disciples that Elijah had come first just as the prophecy said he would "as it is written of him" (Mk 9:13). If the scribes were also Mark's opponents, then he agreed with them that Elijah must come first, but disagreed about whom Elijah was to come before. The scribes claimed that he would come before the Lord God, and Mark argued he would come before the Lord Jesus.

Mark and the scribes also disagreed about whether Elijah had already come. Mark implied that John the Baptist was Elijah, but the scribes believed that Elijah was still to come. This argument about Elijah coming first constituted the structural enthymeme that generated Mark's persuasive discourse. William J. Brandt's book *The Rhetoric of Argumentation* expressed it this way:

> But it should be noted that we are not talking about the relatively simple enthymemes, used by the way, which were discussed in the previous chapter. The enthymeme that constitutes the major argument of an essay will be a structural enthymeme; its parts will constitute a major part of the essay itself, the confirmatio.[1]

The failure of scholars to identify Mark's structural enthymeme was due to their mistranslation of the first word of Mark as "beginning" instead of "guiding principle," and their view of Mark as some kind of story instead of a persuasive speech or argumentative discourse. A good example of this is Vernon K. Robbins' *Jesus the Teacher*, a book in which the author viewed Mark's gospel as a narrative genre and translated its first word as "beginning." In his own words:

> The overall thesis of Mark's gospel is that the gospel of Jesus Christ is the *story* portrayed in the narrative. This thesis is introduced in the opening verse of the document, which claims to be the *beginning* of the gospel of Jesus Christ. (Mk 1:1)[2]

---

1. William J. Brandt, *The Rhetoric of Argumentation*, (Indianapolis/New York: The Bobbs-Merrill Co. Inc., 1970), p. 61.

2. Vernon K. Robbins, *Jesus the Teacher: A Socio-Rhetorical Interpretation of Mark*, (Minneapolis: Fortress Press, 2009), p. 201.

Earlier, he expressed the same view, and described how argumentation proceeded in such a work:

> Since the literary form of Mark's gospel is a narrative rather than a discursive essay, the major theses, demonstrations, and conclusions emerge from the progressive forms that portray Jesus and the disciples.[3]

However, Robbins' description of "a discursive essay" fits Mark better than the above description of "a narrative":

> In a discursive essay, progressive forms result from direct statements by the narrator that assert one or more theses, demonstrate the theses, and draw conclusions from these theses—using brief stories, if the narrator wishes to support or elaborate the theses, demonstrations, or conclusions.[4]

Mark followed this pattern of a discursive essay exactly. Mark 1:1–3 is a *direct statement by the narrator*, in which Mark *asserts the thesis* that God will send his messenger before the Lord to prepare the way. Then Mark *used brief stories* about John the Baptist going before Jesus to *elaborate the thesis and demonstrate the conclusion* that they are the messenger and Lord of the prophecy.

Robbins even reconstructed the syllogism underlying Mark's structural enthymeme as follows:

1. Assertion: *Isaiah* says that God is sending a messenger to prepare the way of the Messiah;

2. Demonstration: John the Baptist comes as a messenger who preaches and announces one mightier than he;

3. Conclusion: therefore, John the Baptist prepares the way of the Messiah.[5]

The most serious objection to Robbins' reconstruction of Mark's introduction is that his translation of arché as "beginning"

3. *Ibid.*, p. 201.
4. *Ibid.*, p. 201.
5. *Ibid.*, p. 201.

The Enthymeme or Rhetorical Syllogism

obliges him to introduce a logical argument with a chronological "beginning," instead of a logical "first principle."

By translating the first word of Mark as "guiding principle," we can see how this principle became the major premise of the structural enthymeme that shaped Mark's persuasive speech. The syllogism underlying this enthymeme can then be reconstructed as follows:

> Major Premise: The guiding principle of the gospel of Jesus Christ (Son of God) is God's promise to send his messenger before the Lord to prepare his way in the desert.
> Minor Premise: John went before Jesus preparing his way in the desert
> Conclusion: Therefore, John is the messenger and Jesus is the Lord.

Writing about the structural enthymeme, William J. Brandt claimed that, "its parts will constitute a major part of the essay itself."[6] I have shown elsewhere in my book, *Mark: A Twice-Told Tale*, how elements of the introduction such as "the way" and "the desert" extend throughout Mark's gospel, which "constitutes" a major part of Mark's "persuasive discourse."[7]

Why Mark told the Story Twice

We have to somehow account for the curious way Mark told the "story" of John the Baptist and Jesus. In the prophecy, they are not named and in the first half of the gospel they are simple called John and Jesus; it is only in the second half of the gospel that they are identified as Elijah and the Son of Man.

For Mark, the clue to the identifies of John and Jesus is found in the order of their appearance—John first, and then Jesus—which corresponded to the order of the appearance of the messenger and the Lord in the prophecy. Therefore, the order of the appearance of

---

6. See reference 1 above.
7. Caurie Beaver, *Mark: A Twice-Told Tale*, pp. 79–83.

John and Jesus was a necessary condition for identifying them as Elijah and the Son of Man, but in itself it was not a sufficient reason for doing so. After all, many had come before Jesus, who were not Elijah, and many came after John the Baptist, who were not the Lord. Something more appears to be required to demonstrate their respective identities. Apparently, Mark was aware of this problem as he set about solving it in a most creative and unusual way—by telling the gospel story twice: once as the story of John and Jesus, and again as the story of Elijah and the Son of Man.

When Mark told the story of John the Baptist, he never called him Elijah, but the description fit that prophet:

> John: "had a leather girdle about his waist" (Mk 1:6).
> Elijah: "with a girdle of leather about his loins" (II Kings 1:8).

It was only when Jesus reflected on the significance of the Baptist's coming first that he identified him as Elijah indirectly. He still did not call John Elijah. The interpretive retelling of the Baptist's story occurred in a dialogue between Jesus and three of his disciples, Peter, James, and John, as they descended the mountain after Jesus' transfiguration.

> And they asked him, "why do the scribes say that first Elijah must come?" and he said to them "Elijah does come first to restore all things; and how is it written of the Son of Man that he should suffer many things and be treated with contempt? But I tell you that Elijah has come and they did to him whatever they pleased as it is written of him" (Mk 9:11–13).

The name John did not occur in this passage; only Matthew made the identification of John the Baptist and Elijah explicit (Matt 17:13). In the re-telling of the story, Mark used the name Elijah, but what he said happened to Elijah fit John the Baptist, who was executed by Herod. Mark nowhere clearly said that John was Elijah; the identification has to be inferred from the way he told the story.

Mark also told the story of Jesus twice: once using the name of Jesus (Mk 1:1—8:30) and again adding the title Son of Man (Mk 8:31—16:8). When Mark wrote about Jesus in the first half of the

The Enthymeme or Rhetorical Syllogism

gospel, the description fit the Son of Man. He attributed to Jesus such miracles as to suggest that he was divine, but the title Son of Man occurred only twice (Mk 2:10, 2:28). Conversely, when Mark wrote about the Son of Man in the second half of the gospel (Mk 8:31, 8:38, 9:9, 9:12, 9:31, 10:33, 10:45, 13:26, 14:21, 14:41, 14:62), the description fit Jesus, who with the disciples, traveled to his death in Jerusalem. But Mark nowhere unequivocally called Jesus the Son of Man. Again, one is obliged to infer Jesus' identity as the Son of Man from the way Mark told the story. It was Matthew who drew the inference and made the identification explicit:

> Gospel of Mark: "who do men say I am?" (Mk 8:27)
> Gospel of Matthew: "who do men say that the Son of Man is?" (Matt 16:13)

The major premise of Mark's structural enthymeme—God promised to send his messenger before the Lord to prepare his way in the desert—coincided with the gospel's introduction (Mk 1:1–3). The minor premise—John went before Jesus preparing his way in the desert—comprised the first half of the gospel (Mk 1:4—8:31). It was only in the middle of the gospel that Mark drew the conclusion that identified John as Elijah and Jesus as the Son of Man. When Jesus agreed with the scribes that Elijah must come first, he alluded to the prophecy at the beginning of the gospel, in which God had promised to send the messenger (Elijah) first, before the Lord. To Mark, it was so obvious what scripture he had in mind that he did not quote it, but referred to it by the quotation formula alone: "as it is written of him," and "how is it written" (Mk 9:11–13).

The scripture that Mark had in mind would also have been obvious to us if we understood the point of the passage in question. Neither the reference to the resurrection, which Wrede focused on, nor the suffering theme to which other scholars drew attention, was the subject of this passage. After the experience on the mountain:

> The entire discussion that followed revolved around the question as to whether it was necessary for Elijah to come first. The disciples asked Jesus why the scribes say

Elijah must come first. In his reply, Jesus answered the disciples by twice referring to the coming first of Elijah: "Elijah is indeed coming first," and "Elijah has come."[8]

Scholars were distracted by the search for a scripture that referred to the suffering of Elijah and overlooked the fact that they already had a scripture that referred to the coming first of Elijah, namely, the messenger prophecy at the beginning of Mark. If, as we have shown, the gospel story were told twice, the messenger prophecy would need to introduce both tellings. When the prophecy introduced the story of John the Baptist and Jesus, Mark quoted it in full, but when the prophecy introduced the story of Elijah and the Son of Man, Mark simply referred to it by the quotation formula, "as it is written."[9] Although he referred to Matthew instead of Mark, Justin Martyr considered this passage the key to the early "Christian" argument for Jesus' messiahship.

How Jesus Revealed to His Disciples that John the Baptist Was Elijah

I will quote in full the passage in which Jesus taught His disciples that John the Baptist was Elijah. (Mk 9:11–13)

> Then they asked him, 'why do the scribes say that Elijah must come first?' He said to them, 'Elijah is indeed coming first to restore all things. *How then is it written about the Son of Man, that he is to go through many sufferings and be treated with contempt*? But I tell you that Elijah has come, and they did to him whatever they pleased, as it is written about him.'

Some scholars consider Mark 9:12b an awkward interpolation.[10] To understand why one merely needs to first read the passage with

---

8. *Ibid.*, p. 78.
9. *Ibid.*, pp. 110–111.
10. Rudolph Bultmann, *The History of the Synoptic Tradition*, Translated by John Marsh, (New York and Evanston, 1963), p. 125. " . . . for I cannot think of the intrusive and unconnected saying about the Son of Man in Mk 9:12b

the "interpolation" and then without it. When one reads the passage (Mk 9:11-13) in isolation, the verse in question (Mk 9:12) does appear to be an awkward insertion. Even Matthew seems to have held this view since he transferred it to a position after the revelation of Elijah's identity. Matthew also omitted the word "first" from the saying about Elijah's coming, which word was required to make Jesus saying an answer to the disciples' question, which was not just about whether Elijah had come but whether he had come first before the Son of Man.

By considering this verse, Mk 9:12b, in its broader context I will show that far from being an awkward interpolation it is an exact fit in the position in which Mark placed it. When Mark told the story of John the Baptist and Jesus in the first half of the gospel, he told it in the order of the prophecy (Mk 1:2-3), the messenger, John the Baptist first then the Lord. But when he revealed their identity as the Son of Man and Elijah, he reversed the order of the prophecy by beginning with the Son of Man. On the Mount of Transfiguration, God called Jesus His beloved Son (Mk 9:7b). Since Jesus had not yet identified John the Baptist as Elijah, His disciples asked him, "Why do the scribes say that Elijah must come first?" (Mk 9:11).

In response to the disciples' question Jesus made a series of statements in the course of which he gradually revealed that John the Baptist was Elijah (Mk 9:12-13). Jesus agreed with the scribes that "Elijah is indeed coming first to restore all things" (Mk 9:12a). He did not say that Elijah had already come, but if Elijah has not come, how can the Son of Man be here or "How then is it written about the Son of Man, that he is to go through many sufferings and be treated with contempt?" (Mk 9:12b). Here Jesus has merely restated the circumstance that prompted the disciples' question in the first place. Then Jesus answered the disciples' question definitively by stating emphatically, "But I tell you that Elijah has come,

---

as anything else than an interpolation. See also Craig A. Evans, *Word Biblical Commentary Vol. 34B, Mark 8:27—16:20*, (Thomas Nelson, Inc., 2001) p. 41. He says in the earliest form of the passage (Mk 9:11-13), the so-called "interpolation" was absent. If the "interpolation" were removed, the disjunctive "but" would need to be changed to a coordinating conjunction "and."

and they did to him whatever they pleased, as it is written about him" (Mk 9:13).

Any doubts about whether the two references to scripture in this passage—"How is it written about the Son of Man..." and "...as it is written about him..."—refer to the prophecy at the beginning of Mark can be finally set aside. They are the only scriptural references in Mark that refer to both John the Baptist and Jesus.

A word is in order about Mark's presentation of Jesus' teachings. In Mark Jesus does not state his views in a straightforward manner. Instead Jesus, His disciples or someone else, asks a question. Then Jesus answers the question, and sometimes a dialogue exchange follows.

A close parallel to the passage we have been discussing can be found in Jesus' teaching in the temple. Even the scribes are mentioned in both passages (Mk 12:35-37). The question: "How can the scribes say that the Messiah is the son of David?" (Mk 12:35b). The answer: then Jesus quotes a psalm in which "The Lord (God) said to my Lord (the Messiah) etc. (Ps 110:1) Jesus concludes with a question:

> David himself calls him (the Messiah) Lord, so how can he be his son?

The final question obviously requires a negative response, the Messiah cannot be the son of David. Out of the hundred or so questions in Mark some will no doubt fit this pattern.

Chapter VII

Elijah Must Come First

The Role of Elijah in Mark's Gospel, the Refutation

THE PROMINENCE OF JOHN the Baptist/Elijah in the Gospel of Mark is a direct result of his role as proof of Jesus' messiahship. By going before Jesus, John the Baptist became the messenger, Elijah, who preceded the Lord in the prophecy. The refutation of this argument, which Mark presented as a refusal to accept the identification of John the Baptist as Elijah, is a mirror image of the gospel's argument for Jesus' messiahship. When the people failed to accept John as Elijah, they also refused to accept Jesus as the Messiah.

The form this refutation assumed in Mark is virtually identical to the way it was presented in Justin Martyr's, *Dialogue with Trypho the Jew*, in the second century:

> And Trypho said, "You seem to me to be ready to answer any of my questions, thanks to your extensive exchange in debates with the many persons on every possible topic.[1]

One of the topics was the coming first of Elijah. "Trypho says, '. . .from the fact that Elijah has not yet come, I must declare that

---

1. St. Justin Martyr, *Dialogue with Trypho*, Translated by Thomas B. Falls, revised with a new introduction by Thomas P. Halton, edited by Michael Slusser, (Washington D.C.: The Catholic University: Press of America, 2003), p. 76.

this man (Jesus) is not the Christ."[2] When he answered Trypho, Justin Martyr cited a parallel passage in Matthew in which the identification of John the Baptist with Elijah is stated explicitly, whereas in Mark it is only alluded to obscurely:

> Wherefore did our Christ, who was on earth at this time, reply to those who were saying that Elijah must come before the appearance of Christ, "Elijah indeed is to come and will restore all things. But I say to you that Elijah has come already and they did not know him, but did to him whatever they wished. And it is added, then the disciples understood that he had spoken to them of John the Baptist."[3]

When Mark's Jesus mentioned the resurrection on the mountain, the disciples objected saying, "Why do the scribes say Elijah must come first?" (Mk 9:9–13). Although elsewhere Mark said Jesus taught with authority and not as the scribes (Mk 1:22), here Jesus agreed with them as to the necessity of the coming first of Elijah. Where Mark's Jesus differed with them was on the question as to whether Elijah had already come in the person of John the Baptist, but the scribes did not accept this identification of John with Elijah. Failure to do so constituted a denial that Jesus was the messiah in accordance with the principle that Elijah must come first.

This principle may also explain a peculiarity in the scene on the mountain. Mark wrote, "and there appeared to them Elijah with Moses, who were talking with Jesus (Mk 9:4)." The problem is that Elijah lived sometime after Moses, and is here mentioned before him. Since Moses was sometimes considered a Messianic figure, Mark could not allow him to appear before Elijah; Matthew restored the chronological order, Moses then Elijah, "Suddenly there appeared to them Moses and Elijah talking with him" (Matt 17:3).

Another passage in Mark shows that he was aware of the Deuteronomic promise of the coming of a prophet like unto Moses. The passage in Deuteronomy reads:

---

2. *Ibid.*, p. 74.
3. *Ibid.*, p. 75.

Elijah Must Come First

Moses continued, "The Lord your God will raise up for you a prophet like me from among your fellow Israelites. You must listen to him" (Deut. 18:15).

The passage in Mark reads:

> Then a cloud overshadowed them, and from the cloud there came a voice, "This is my Son the Beloved, *listen to him*" (Mk 9:7).

Since Mark knew that Moses lived before Elijah, did he create a scene in which Moses appeared after Elijah in accordance with his guiding principle that Elijah must come first?

Moreover, the scribes were not the only ones who failed to recognize that John the Baptist was Elijah. Mark mentioned Elijah in other contexts that implied that many people also rejected this identification. When Jesus sent his disciples to preach, cast out demons, and heal the sick:

> King Herod heard of it for Jesus' name had become known. Some were saying "John the baptizer has been raised from the dead; and for this reason these powers are at work in him." But others said, "It is Elijah," and others said, "It is a prophet like one of the prophets of old." But when Herod heard of it he said, "John, whom I beheaded, has been raised" (Mk 6:12–16).

In any case, this would preclude the identification of John the Baptist with Elijah and Jesus with the Messiah. Similarly, when Jesus asked his disciples on the way to Caesarea Philippi, "'who do people say I am?' And they answered him, 'John the Baptist; and others, Elijah; and still others, one of the prophets'" (Mk 8:27–28). Therefore, the same conclusion can be drawn, namely, that the people still did not consider John the Baptist Elijah or Jesus the Messiah.

The next challenge to Jesus' Messiahship came in the temple, which Jesus had just "cleansed."

> And when the chief priests and the scribes heard it, they kept looking for a way to kill him; for they were afraid

of him, because the whole crowd was spellbound by his teaching (Mk 11:18).

When Jesus returned to Jerusalem and to the temple, the chief priests, scribes, and elders challenged his authority when they said, "by what authority are you doing these things? Who gave you this authority to do them?"

This time, they are not accusing him of working with Beelzebub, the ruler of demons. They appear to have in mind human rulers, the Romans, the source of their own authority. Jesus called their attention to the divine source of his own authority by alluding to heaven as the source of John the Baptist's authority.

> "Jesus said to them, 'I will ask you one question; answer me and I will tell you by what authority I do these things. Did the baptism of John come from heaven, or was it of human origin? Answer me.' They agreed with one another, "If we say 'from heaven' he will say "Why then did you not believe him? But shall we say 'Of human origin?'—they were afraid of the crowd, for all regarded John as truly a prophet"—but not Elijah—"So they answered Jesus, "We do not know. And Jesus said to them, 'Neither will I tell you by what authority I am doing these things'" (Mk 11:27–33).

It is obvious that Jesus was referring to John the Baptist's role as the messenger, Elijah, who came before him and prepared his way. By rejecting the heavenly origin and divine source of John's authority the Jerusalem leaders were also rejecting Jesus' Messiahship because John the Baptist/Elijah must come first.

Finally Mark introduced the Elijah issue into the crucifixion scene:

> At three o'clock, Jesus cried out with a loud voice, "Eloi, Eloi, lema sabachthani?" which means, "My God, My God, why have you forsaken me?" When some of the bystanders heard it, they said, "Listen, he is calling for Elijah . . . wait, let us see whether Elijah will come to take him down" (Mk 15:34–36).

Apologetic interests have so dominated the interpretation of this verse that some have suggested that Jesus quoted the entire

Elijah Must Come First

Psalm 22 from which this saying was taken, which ended on a positive note.

Those who still believe in the trinity must wonder how God could forsake himself. The Gnostics solved the problem by separating the divine Christ from the man Jesus, allowing Christ to escape as Jesus died on the cross.[4]

Both of these solutions, in my opinion, miss Mark's point, which is contained in what the people heard, not in what Jesus said. Instead of "My God, My God, why have you forsaken me," they heard, "Elijah, Elijah, why have you forsaken me?" If Jesus were calling for Elijah, as the bystanders thought, he could not have been the Messiah, because Elijah must come first. According to Mark:

> when some of the bystanders heard Jesus' cry, they said "Listen, he is calling Elijah" and someone ran, filled a sponge with sour wine, put it on a stick, and gave it to him to drink, saying "wait, let us see whether Elijah will come to take him down" (Mk 15:35–36).

From these examples, we can see that the people in Mark did not accept his argument for Jesus' Messiahship. But what about the other gospel writers? How did they respond to Mark's argument and were they convinced by it? Whether he understood Mark's reasoning, for the most part Matthew accepted his conclusion that Jesus was the Christ adding that he was also the Son of David. Luke even had John the Baptist precede Jesus in birth (Lk 1:30–38). This brings us to the Gospel of John, which shared with Mark the key word arché and an unusual preoccupation with John "the Baptist," but denied that he was Elijah, and rejected Mark's key principle, the return of Elijah.

---

4. Bart Ehrman, *Last Christianities: The Battles for Scriptures and the Faiths We Never Knew*, (Oxford University Press, 2003), p. 15.

Chapter VIII

The Logos Must Come First
The Role of John "the Baptist" in John's Gospel

After Me: Was Mark's Jesus a Disciple of John the Baptist?

THE GUIDING PRINCIPLE OF Mark's gospel, requiring that Elijah come first, did grant to John the Baptist a certain degree of priority. Almost everything Mark wrote about John the Baptist/Elijah underscored the point: John appeared in the wilderness baptizing and preaching *before* Jesus came from Galilee to be baptized by him. John the Baptist referred to Jesus as the one who would come *after* him; Jesus returned to Galilee to begin his ministry only *after* John was delivered up. Finally, John the Baptist's imprisonment and subsequent execution by Herod insured that Jesus' ministry would continue only *after* John the Baptist was removed from the scene completely, leaving no possibility that their ministries would overlap. However, in the Gospel of John their ministries did overlap as the following passage makes clear.

> "After this Jesus and his disciples went into the Judean countryside (land) and he spent some time there with them and baptized. John also was baptizing at Aenon near Salim because *water was abundant there*; and people

kept coming and were being baptized—John, of course, had not yet been thrown into prison" (Jn. 3:22b-23).

It does not say that Jesus was baptizing with water and earlier John the Baptist had said that he (Jesus) baptized with the Holy Spirit:

> "And John testified, 'I saw the Spirit descending from heaven like a dove, and it remained on him. I myself did not know him, but the one who sent me to baptize with water said to me, 'He on whom you see the Spirit descend and remain is the one who baptized with the Holy Spirit'" (Jn. 1:32–33).

In the passage above that has Jesus baptizing it says that he and his disciples went into "the Judean *land*;" there is no mention of water, so it is tempting to suggest that he was baptizing with the Holy Spirit. This contrasted with the description of the place where John the Baptist was baptizing, "*water was abundant there!*" Of course John was sent "to baptize with water." Another passage may imply that Jesus' disciples continued to baptize with water:

> Now when Jesus learned that the Pharisees had heard, "Jesus is making and baptizing more disciples than John," [although it was not Jesus, himself, but his disciples who baptized] he left Judea and started back to Galilee (Jn. 4:1–3).

According to Walter Wink:

> The problem of Jesus' subordination to John, both as a disciple and at baptism, had already brought forth a variety of solutions. The Fourth Evangelist's is perhaps the simplest and safest: Jesus is baptized before the narrative begins.[1]

However, nowhere did the Fourth Gospel indicate that Jesus was baptized in water by John the Baptist or anyone else. Wink's assumption that the Baptist baptized Jesus before the narrative

---

1. Walter Wink, *John the Baptist in Gospel Tradition* (Reprinted by Wipf and Stock Publishers, Eugene, OR, 2000), p. 104. Previously published by Cambridge University Press, 1968).

began is very doubtful. When he concluded that, "In the same, absolute sense as in Mark, John is still the beginning of the Gospel" (Jn. 1:6–8, 19ff), he said the opposite of what the Fourth Gospel claims. For John's gospel, the Logos was the beginning of the gospel not John the Baptist.[2]

John's gospel did not even tell the story of John the Baptist's death, possibly out of a fear that it would be viewed as a sacrificial death and upstage the sacrificial death of Jesus, the Lamb of God. The closest he came to reporting the Baptist's death was in the comment, "John, of course, had not yet been thrown into prison," and "He must increase, but I must decrease" (Jn. 3:24, 30).

Some scholar have noticed that Mark's story of John the Baptist's death with the presentation of the Baptist's severed head at Herod's banquet constituted a grotesque Last Supper with the head of John the Baptist instead of the body of Christ as the main course.[3] Elsewhere, Wink expressed the relationship of the Baptist to Jesus more accurately:

> "The Evangelist also sharply contradicts the earlier tradition that John was Elijah. For him the idea of a forerunner is anathema; notice how carefully he has already applied the antidote to it in John 1:1, 15. John is not the forerunner, for the Logos is already first (*protos*) (Jn. 1:15, 30) and can have no forerunner."[4]

In his effort to conform the appearance of John the Baptist and Jesus to the messenger prophecy, Mark inadvertently introduced a problem. Mark had the Baptist proclaim, "The one who is more powerful than I is coming after me (opiso mou) (Mk 1:7). Mark's choice of words is ambiguous. The Baptist/Mark may have meant the words in a purely chronological sense, but "coming after" someone can signify following them as that person's disciple.

---

2. *Ibid.*, p. 106.

3. Janice Capel Anderson and Stephen D. Moore, editors, *Mark and Method: New Approaches in Biblical Studies* (Minneapolis: Fortress Press, 1992), p. 132.

4. Walter Wink, *John the Baptist in the Gospel Tradition*, p. 89.

The Logos Must Come First

When Jesus called his first disciples, he used the same expression, "come after me," in the imperative of course (Mk 1:17).

The author of the Gospel of John was no doubt responding to just this problem in Mark when he revised the Baptist's statement giving rise to the most complicated riddle in that gospel of riddles.[5] The author of the Gospel of John quoted the Baptist as saying, "This was he of whom I said, 'He who comes after me ranks ahead of me because he was before me'" (Jn. 1:15). As if he were afraid the reader/hearer would miss the point, the author of the Fourth Gospel had the Baptist repeat the statement almost word for word, "After me comes a man who ranks ahead of me because he was before me" (Jn. 1:30).

By saying this, the author of the Fourth Gospel was denying that Jesus was a follower of the Baptist and inferior to him. The solution to the riddle is simple—in his incarnated state Jesus came after the Baptist, but he outranked the Baptist because he preceded him in his pre-incarnated state as the Logos in the beginning with God. In other words, the Logos must come first.[6]

When I claim that the author of the Gospel of John was reacting to Mark's apparent high estimate of John the Baptist, I do not stand alone. After quoting the messenger prophecy in Mark, Nigel Turner wrote:

> Such an interpretation puts the claims of John (the Baptist) very high. He announces the Messiah. More; he is part of the gospel itself. It is an exalted image, which may have assumed dangerous proportions, and the statements in Chapter 1 of St. John's gospel look very like an attempt to revise the depiction.[7]

---

5. Tom Thatcher, *The Riddles of Jesus in John, A Study in Tradition and Folklore*, (Atlanta, GA: Society of Biblical Literature, 2000), p. 184. See also Pere M. Phillips, *The Prologue of the Fourth Gospel: A Sequential Reading*, (London: T&T Clark, 2006), pp. 209, 210.

6. Adele Reinhartz, *The Word in the World: The Cosmological Tale in the Fourth Gospel*, (Atlanta, GA: Scholars Press, 1992), *passim*. Reinhartz's book provides the context for the above solution to the riddle of Jn. 1:30.

7. Nigel Turner, *Grammatical Insights into the New Testament*, p. 28.

In this first instance Turner was led by a consideration of the messenger prophecy's content to a correct intuition. Mark did appear to place the arché, or guiding principle of the gospel of Jesus Christ at John the Baptist. In contrast, John's gospel placed the arché at the Logos in the beginning with God. Then Turner wrote:

> "Bind together verses 1 and 4 and regard the intervening matter as parenthesis. It will read like this. "John the Baptist baptizing . . . and preaching . . . was the beginning of the gospel of Jesus Christ." This simple and clear statement was in the evangelist's mind as he took his pen, but a complicating parenthesis occurred to him as he began to write. Somewhere we must insert: 'As it is written in the prophets [sic] Behold I sent my messenger before thy face.'"[8]

In other words, Mark's description of the Baptist's role as the forerunner of the Messiah is viewed as an afterthought expressed in the form of a parenthesis. In this second instance, Turner was led by a consideration of syntax to an erroneous conclusion. What is even more astonishing, Turner went on to characterize the messenger prophecy as a "footnote"! Little did he realize that the prophecy was for Mark a programmatic statement of his purpose.[9]

Arché in John's Gospel : When does the Beginning Begin?

It is customary for books on Mark to compare Mark 1:1, "(the) Beginning of the gospel of Jesus Christ" to John 1:1, "in the beginning was the word," and Genesis 1:1, "in the beginning God created." The translation of arché in Mark 1:1 as "guiding principle" instead of "beginning" clarifies the relationship among these three passages. Scholars have read Mark 1:1, which does not refer to Genesis 1:1, through the lens of John 1:1, which does. If Mark had intended to refer to Genesis 1:1, he had another phrase available to

---

8. *Ibid.*, p. 28.
9. *Ibid.*, p. 28.

The Logos Must Come First

him, "(the) beginning of creation" (Mk 10:6, 13:9), which he used elsewhere.

It is probably no accident that Mark and John began their gospel with the same word—arché. They also share an unusual preoccupation with John the Baptist. However, their treatment of him is quite different. Mark described the Baptist as the prophet Elijah, and the forerunner of the Messiah, who went ahead of him and prepared his way. He even dared to draw a parallel between the suffering of John the Baptist, Elijah and that of Jesus, the Son of Man. If the Baptist was delivered up, the Son of Man was also delivered up. Whereas Mark's gospel placed its guiding principle, arché at the messenger prophecy, John's gospel placed its rational principle, the logos, at the beginning with God before creation. In fact, John's gospel attributed all three meaning of arché to Jesus, "In the beginning (chronological priority) was the word, (logical priority) and the word was with God, and the word was God (ultimate ruling authority)" (Jn. 1:1).[10]

In Mark's gospel God sent John the Baptist/Elijah before Jesus, which conferred on him chronological priority and appeared to also grant him personal superiority. When John's gospel identified Jesus as the Logos with God in the beginning, Jesus, as the Logos—God, became the one who sent the Baptist. By placing the Logos—God in the beginning, John's gospel at one stroke denied to the Baptist both chronological priority and superior personal authority. This claim to chronological priority and divinity is found in Jesus' own words in John's gospel:

> Your ancestor Abraham rejoiced that he would see my day; he saw it and was glad. Then the Jews said to him, "You are not yet 50 years old, and have you seen Abraham?" Jesus said to them, "Very truly, I tell you before Abraham was, I am" (Jn. 8:56–58).

---

10. A. M. Hunter, *The Gospel According to John*, The Cambridge Biblical Community on the New English Bible (Cambridge at the University Press, 1965), p. 15, 16. Hunter says en arché, "in the beginning" can also mean "in principle."

Johannine scholars recognize that the "I am" sayings in John's gospel constitute a transparent claim to divine status: "I am the bread of life 9); before Abraham was, I am (8:58); I am the door (10:7, 9); I am the good shepherd (10:11), I am the resurrection and the life (11:25), I am the way, the truth, and the life (14:6), and I am the true vine (15:1).[11]

When God summoned Moses to deliver his people from Egypt, Moses said that the people would want to know who sent him. God replied, "say to this people Israel: 'I am has sent me to you" (Ex 3:13, 14). We have already seen how God's introduction to Moses at the burning bush figured in Jesus' argument for the resurrection. God said to Moses, "I am the God of your ancestors—the God of Abraham, the God of Isaac, and the God of Jacob" (Exo 3:15).

John's gospel proceeded simultaneously to promote Jesus and systematically demote John the Baptist. In direct contradiction to Mark, John's gospel had the Baptist deny that he was Elijah in a passage in which the Baptist stripped himself of almost every other honorific title including the Messiah and the prophet.

> This is the testimony given by John when the Jews sent priests and Levites from Jerusalem to ask him, "Who are you?" He confessed and did not deny it, but confessed, "I am not the Messiah" and they asked him, "what then? Are you Elijah?" He said, "I am not." "Are you the prophet?" He answered, "No." Then they said to him, "Who are you? Let us have an answer for those who sent us. What do you say about yourself?" he said, "I am the voice of one crying in the wilderness, 'make straight the way of the Lord,' as the prophet Isaiah said" (Jn. 1:19–23).

It may even be significant that the gospel's Greek reads only "I (a) voice" instead of "I am (a) voice." By omitting "I am," the gospel avoided even a hint of a divine John the Baptist. Otherwise, "I am" occurs in a negative statement in which John the Baptist says, "I am not the Christ" (Jn. 1:20). When he denied being the Christ

---

11. Adele Reinhartz, *The Word in the World*, pp. 34, 35.

a second time, John the Baptist again reversed the two terms in question, "not am I the Christ" (Jn. 3:28).[12]

Did John Know Mark's Gospel?
All Who Came Before Me

Before Percival Gardner-Smith's book, *Saint John and the Synoptic Gospels*, it was considered likely that John was aware of the Synoptic gospels, "certainly knew Mark, probably knew Luke, and possibly knew Matthew."[13] After Gardner-Smith's book, it became fashionable to deny that John knew the Synoptic Gospels.[14] However, Smith wrote before redaction (editorial) and literary criticism revealed the different theologies of the four canonical gospels. Prior to these holistic studies of the gospels, influence usually meant agreement in words or thought. Now that we know that the gospels' theologies differ, influence can involve disagreement, ranging from minor changes to radical revision or even outright opposition.[15]

The relationship between Mark's gospel and John's can best be seen in their respective treatments of the career of John the Baptist. The role of the Baptist in the Gospel of John is a virtual mirror image of the role of Elijah in the Gospel of Mark. What Mark affirmed, John denied. In both cases, their reasoning was shaped by a guiding principle, which in Mark was the coming first of Elijah, and in John, the absolute priority of the Logos. In Mark's gospel, Jesus arrived on the scene after God sent John the Baptist to baptize and preach; in John's gospel, God sent the "Baptist," "to

---

12. Lane C. McGaughy, *A Descriptive Analysis of Einai as a Linking Verb in New Testament Greek* (Society of Biblical Literature, Dissertation Series, Number six, 1972) pp. 142, 143.

13. Percival Gardner-Smith, *Saint John and the Synoptic Gospels*, (Cambridge: Cambridge University Press, 1938), *passim*.

14. D. Moody Smith, *John Among the Gospels*, (Minneapolis: Fortress Press, 1992), p. 85.

15. Donald Foster, *The Bible and the Narrative Tradition*, Ed. by Frank McConnell, "John Come Lately: The Belated Evangelist," (New York: Oxford University Press, 1986), p. 113.

testify to the light" (Jn. 1:6) after the light had already shined in the darkness (Jn. 1:5), which foreshadowed the incarnation.

Mark's introduction began with the word, arché, the "guiding principle," which was the coming first of the messenger, John the Baptist, Elijah. After this brief introduction (Mk 1:1-3), the Baptist appeared in the wilderness. John's gospel introduction also began with the word arché, the "guiding principle," which was the coming first of the Logos, "the true light which enlightens everyone" (Jn. 1:9). After this brief introduction, God sent John, not to prepare the way of the Lord, but to testify to his previous arrival in the world.

Mark derived the order of John and Jesus' appearance from a messianic interpretation of the messenger prophecy (Mk 1:2-3) and made it the guiding principle of his argument for Jesus' messiahship. In my opinion this succession John/Elijah then Jesus/Son of Man was the outcome of Mark's own rhetorical argument and was not derived from an earlier "Christian" or Jewish tradition. Mark had John the Baptist assert, "the one who is more powerful than I is coming *after me*" (Mk 1:7). John's gospel had the Baptist assert just the opposite, "after me comes a man who ranks ahead of me because he was *before me*" (Jn. 1:30).

In Mark, John the Baptist says nothing about Jesus being before him. If Mark had allowed Jesus to appear before John the Baptist, it would have invalidated his guiding principle requiring that Elijah come first. According to Donald Foster, John went so far as to claim that his gospel contained *the* truth. His motto was: "I (Jesus/John's Gospel) am the way, the truth, and the life" (Jn. 14:6). John also claimed, "I (Jesus/John's Gospel) am the gate for the sheep. All who came before me (Matthew, Mark, and Luke) are thieves and bandits" (Jn. 10:7b-8).[16]

So superior was this message of John's gospel that it could not be contained in the simple, literal narrative of the synoptic gospels, but required instead a completely different form of discourse, sometimes characterized as divine revelations. The double

---

16. George Johnston, *The Spirit Paraclete in the Gospel of John*, (Cambridge: At the University Press, 1970), p. 141.

meanings in which John's gospel abounds were a direct consequence of this exalted vision. For example, when Jesus spoke about salvation in terms of birth, Nicodemus thought about natural birth and asked Jesus how it was possible to be "born again," but Jesus had only spoken about being "born from above" not born again. Those who are born again are Nicodemus' disciples in their misunderstanding of Jesus' spiritual message.

The Paraclete, The Angelic Reminder

Another notion in the Gospel of John that has some bearing on the relationship of John to the Synoptic Gospels is that of the Paraclete, who, after Jesus is gone, will come and remind his disciples of all that he had taught them.

> I have said these things while I am still with you. But the advocate (paraclete), the Holy Spirit whom the Father will send in my name will teach you everything, and remind you of all that I have said to you (Jn. 14:25, 26).

By translating "paraclete" as "advocate," the Revised Standard Version has emphasized the forensic role of the paraclete. I prefer to call attention to his role as teacher, interpreter, and reminder. Then John says that Jesus spoke about things that the disciples did not understand at the time, but would understand later and "remember" what he taught them. "But I have said these things to you so that when the hour comes you may remember that I told you about them" (Jn. 16:4).

Then there were things held back because the disciples were not yet ready to hear them, but the "Spirit of the Truth" will later deliver these teachings to the disciples. Here it is no longer a matter of remembering what Jesus taught the disciples, but the Spirit of Truth adding to what he taught. "I still have many things to say to you, but you cannot bear them now. When the Spirit of Truth comes, he will guide you into all the truth" (Jn. 16:12–13).

Just what teachings of Jesus was the paraclete reminding the disciples of, what will they "remember" and understand later, and what is "all the truth" that the Spirit will guide them into? The naïve view is that the paraclete would bring to the remembrance of the disciples the teachings of the historical Jesus as recorded in the synoptic gospels, Matthew, Mark, and Luke. It is much more likely, however, that the "remembered" teachings are the ones found in the Gospel of John itself.

Hans Windisch had this to say about these "remembered" teachings:

> "Here we find one of the few passages in John (Jn. 14:25, 26) that could be said to sanction the older gospel tradition. However, within the framework of the Fourth Gospel, with its claim to sufficiency, its autonomy, and its usually thoroughgoing negation of the older writings, it is more accurate to relate the words, "He will . . . bring to your remembrance all that I have said to you" to the tradition extant in the Fourth Gospel."[17]

Wrede's Notion of the Post-Resurrection Enlightenment of the Disciples

These "remembered" teachings could also be related to William Wrede's notion of the post-resurrection enlightenment of the disciples. After using this idea to interpret Mark's gospel, Wrede made an astonishing admission that the notion is found nowhere in Mark, but only in the Gospel of John. Wrede put it this way:

> " . . . he (John) expressly singles out the resurrection as the decisive moment in time. This Mark nowhere did in statements about the disciples. Nevertheless I have interpreted him in the light of this idea."[18]

---

17. Hans Windisch, *The Spirit Paraclete in the Fourth Gospel*, (Philadelphia: Fortress Press, 1968), p. 7. Translated by James W. Cox. First published as "Die fiinf johanneischen Para-Kletspriiche," in Festgabe fur Adolf Julicher (Tubigen: J. C. B. Mohr, Paul Siebeck, 1927).

18. William Wrede, *The Messianic Secret*, Translated by J. C. G. Greig, (James Clark and Co. LTD: Cambridge and London, 1971), p. 186.

Whereas Mark told the story of John the Baptist and Jesus and then interpreted it as the story of Elijah and the Son of Man, in John's gospel interpretation almost completely absorbed and displaced the story of Jesus, revelatory discourse replaced narrative. While Mark's story of Jesus is that of a man whose excellence as a teacher, skill as a debater, performer of wonders and obedient to God's will merited his becoming God's son at his death, John's story of Jesus was that of a God whose teachings could only be grasped with the help of an angelic interpretation, the Paraclete.

What George Kennedy said about Mark's use of "sacred language" to assert, "absolute claim of authoritative truth without evidence or logical argument" could with greater justification be applied to the Gospel of John.[19] John's gospel stakes a claim to the truth that is so absolute and exclusive as to preclude debate about its validity. While Mark's Jesus submitted his view to argumentation and debate, John's gospel portrayed Jesus' teaching as light shining in darkness and the darkness as uncomprehending and unable to overcome it. What in Mark was portrayed as an intellectual contest between Jesus and his opponents, in John's gospel became an all-out power struggled between light and darkness.

---

19. George A. Kennedy, *New Testament Interpretation through Rhetorical Criticism* (Chapel Hill: University of North Carolina Press, 1984).

Chapter IX

Conclusion

The Guiding Principle of Mark's Gospel: Elijah Must Come First

Introduction

ACCORDING TO ALBERT SCHWEITZER in the time of Jesus the Jews were expecting the appearance, not of the Messiah, but Elijah, the forerunner.[1] Superficially read, the evidence appears to support Schweitzer's view. When Jesus' name became known through the preaching of the Twelve, the people believed that he was John the Baptist, Elijah, or one of the prophets. The conscience ridden King Herod thought Jesus was John the Baptist whom he had beheaded (Mk. 6:14–16). When Jesus at Caesarea Philippi asked the disciples, "Who do people say that I am?" They answered, "John the Baptist; and others, Elijah; and still others, one of the prophets" (Mk. 8:27–30). Since no proportions are given one cannot conclude from these passages how widespread each belief was.

Some scholars have recently called into question the notion that the belief that Elijah would be the forerunner of the Messiah was widely held by the Jews in the time of Jesus. They point out

---

1. Albert Schweitzer, *The Mystery of the Kingdom of God*, (New York: The Macmillan Company, 1957), p. 83.

CONCLUSION

how little evidence there is for it outside the gospels.[2] Since the notion in Mark arises from messianic speculation, it may not be found among non-messianic Jews. The belief in the return of Elijah is based on a messianic reading of a passage in the last book of the Old Testament, "Lo, I will send you the prophet Elijah before the great and terrible day of the LORD comes." (Mal. 4:4)

Non-messianic Jewish exegesis took this passage to mean that Elijah would return before the Day of the LORD God; messianic interpretation concluded that Elijah would return before the Day of the LORD Jesus. Mark may have been right when he attributed to the scribes the belief in the return of Elijah before the End time, but it was probably Mark and his community who made Elijah the messenger and forerunner of the Messiah (Mk. 9:11).

For Mark the return of Elijah was the guiding principle of the gospel which necessarily preceded the question of Christology, for if Elijah had not come, Jesus was simply not the Messiah. Any doubting or denying that Elijah had come constituted a questioning or rejecting of Jesus' messiahship. Just as Elijah must come first, Mark must first establish that Elijah has already come. That is why Mark's gospel began with the messenger prophecy (Mk. 1:2-3). The principle of the return of Elijah was so important to Mark that he repeated it twice in the messenger prophecy, placed Elijah before Moses at the Transfiguration (Mk. 9:4), explained it to the three disciples as they descended the mountain (Mk. 9:9-13), and even mentioned Elijah in the crucifixion scene in which bystanders heard Jesus say, "Elijah, Elijah, why have you forsaken me?" (Mk. 15:34).

When Mark attributed the belief in the return of Elijah to the scribes, he began to reveal the conclusions he had drawn from this "guiding principle" (arché) of the gospel. In other references to Elijah Mark demonstrated that the people consistently rejected Jesus' equation of John the Baptist with Elijah, and also rejected Jesus' messianic claims.

In order to show how this "debate" determined the form of Mark's argument and generated the structure of the gospel, it will

---

2. Faierstein, Morris M. "Why Do the Scribes Say That Elijah Comes First?" JBL 100 (1981) 75-86.

be necessary to offer a revision of the first three verses of Mark, and suggest that they constitute the introduction to his persuasive discourse. This introduction will then be compared to the prooemium of that other persuasive discourse or word of exhortation, the book of Hebrews (Heb. 1:1–4).

Mark's / Jesus' "Debate" With The Scribes: Has Elijah Already Come?

> "As they were coming down the mountain, he ordered them to tell no one about what they had seen, until after the Son of Man had risen from the dead. So they kept the matter to themselves, questioning what this rising from the dead could mean. Then they asked him, 'Why do the scribes say that Elijah must come first?' He said to them, 'Elijah is indeed coming first to restore all things. How then is it written about the Son of Man, that he is to go through many sufferings and be treated with contempt? But I tell you that Elijah has come, and they did to him whatever they pleased, as it is written about him'" (Mk. 9:9–13).

The opinion that Mark had Jesus' disciples attribute to the scribes constituted a denial that Jesus was the Messiah because Elijah had not yet come. Since Mark / Jesus agreed with the scribes that Elijah must come first, the "debate" was about whether Elijah had already come. Mark / Jesus argued that John the Baptist was Elijah, but throughout the gospel the scribes and others refused to accept this identification. Even Jesus' own disciples quoted the scribes' objection to what Jesus had just said, and Mark, unlike Matthew, did not say that they understood after Jesus' explanation.

One gets the impression that Matthew objected to Mark's account on the basis of both form and content. Leaving aside Matthew's stylistic changes, we will concentrate only on those of substance. In Mark's account of the Transfiguration Elijah was mentioned before Moses (Mk. 9:4); In Matthew's account Moses was placed first before Elijah restoring their chronological order

Conclusion

(Matt. 17:3). When Jesus replied to the disciples' question about the scribal tradition, he said, "Elijah has come," and Matthew added, "and they did not recognize him" (Matt. 17:12). Matthew understood that Jesus was speaking about John the Baptist, but he noticed that Mark had not said that the disciples understood. This left the impression that the disciples remained on the side of the scribes, who did not consider John Elijah. Therefore, Matthew added, "Then the disciples understood that he was speaking to them about John the Baptist" (Matt. 17:13). Matthew clearly spelled out that "they," the scribes, did not consider John the Baptist Elijah, but that the disciples did.

In the second century the subject of the return of Elijah resurfaced in St. Justin Martyr's *Dialogue with Trypho*, the Jew.

> "And Trypho said, 'You seem to me to be ready to answer any of my questions, thanks to your extensive exchange in debates with many persons on every possible topic.[3]

One of the topics was the return of Elijah.

> Trypho says, "...from the fact that Elijah has not yet come, I must declare that this man (Jesus) is not the Christ."[4]

Justin Martyr answered,

> Wherefore did our Christ, who was on earth at this time, reply to those who were saying that Elijah must come before the appearance of Christ, 'Elijah indeed is to come and will restore all things. But I say to you that Elijah has come already, and they did not know him, but did to him whatever they wished. And it is added, Then the disciples understood that he had spoken to them of John the Baptist.[5]

The scribes were not the only ones who failed to recognize that John the Baptist was Elijah. Elijah is mentioned in contexts

---

3. St. Justin Martyr, *Dialogue With Trypho*, Tr. By Thomas B. Falls, Revised and with a New Introduction by Thomas P. Halton, Ed. By Michael Slusser, (Washington D.C.: The Catholic Univ. Press of America, 2003), p. 76.

4. *Ibid.*, p. 74.

5. *Ibid.*, p. 75.

that imply that the people also reject this identification. When Herod heard about Jesus, he thought that he was John the Baptist raised from the dead. The people thought he was John the Baptist, Elijah, or one of the prophets. In any case this would tend to negate the identification of John the Baptist with Elijah (Mk. 6:14–15). Similarly, when Jesus asked the disciples on the way to Caesarea Philippi, "Who do people say that I am?", their reply was virtually identical to the opinions of the people when Herod heard about Jesus (Mk. 8:27–28). Therefore, the same conclusion can be drawn, namely, that the people did not consider John the Baptist Elijah.

Again in the Temple when the Jewish leaders were questioning Jesus' authority, and Jesus challenged them to declare themselves in regard to John's baptism, they refused. They would not say John's baptism was of human origin for fear of the people. Then Mark added, "for all regarded John as truly a prophet" (Mk. 11:32), but not Elijah!

Finally, Mark introduced the Elijah issue into the crucifixion scene. In Mark Jesus cried from the cross, "My God, My God, why have you forsaken me?" (Mk. 15:34). Apologetic interests have so dominated the interpretation of this verse that some have suggested that Jesus quoted the entire Psalm 22 from which this saying was taken, which ended on a positive note. However, if we read the saying in the context of the gospel of Mark, we realize that Mark focused on a seemingly irrelevant misunderstanding on the part of the people gathered around the cross. Because of the similarity of sounds in the original languages in the place of "My God, My God, why have you forsaken me?", the people heard, "Elijah, Elijah, why have you forsaken me?" If Mark created this scene, as I believe he did, this misunderstanding and not Psalm 22 may contain the point he was making. Once again, if the people thought that Elijah might "come to take him down" from the cross, they did not consider John Elijah (Mk. 15:34–36).

In the dialogue that followed the Transfiguration Jesus referred to the scriptures twice—"how then is it written," and "as it is written about him" (Mk. 9:12–13)—but no quotations followed. Elsewhere I argued that both references were to the messenger

Conclusion

prophecy at the beginning of Mark.[6] A more convincing argument for a link between the prophecy and the dialogue is their common subject. If the subject of the conversation between Jesus and his disciples on descending the mountain of Transfiguration was the return of Elijah, then the references in it to unspecified scriptures were to the messenger prophecy, because the return of Elijah was also the subject of that prophecy.

Scholars have usually understood the messenger prophecy (Mk. 1:2–3) in terms of a prophecy and its fulfillment, but in the context of the debate with the scribes it assumed the form of an argument for Jesus' messiahship. Therefore, for Mark the return of Elijah became "The guiding principle (arché) of the gospel of Jesus Christ, Son of God."(Mk. 1:1). The importance this principle had for Mark is unmistakable in that he repeated it four times: in the messenger prophecy he has the messenger / you, and the voice / Lord; in the following narrative John / Jesus and in the above dialogue Elijah / Son of Man.

Mark Answers the Scribes: John Was Elijah

When Mark had Jesus explain to his disciples that Elijah had come first, he presented a conclusion to a tightly reasoned argument that began with the first word of Mark, arché, which is usually translated beginning. Translators believed that Mark intended arché to refer to the beginning of the gospel story; in contrast we will translate arché as "(The) guiding principle" and take it to indicate the starting-point of a reasoned discourse. In another move translators put a period after the first line of Mark and consider it the title of the gospel. We will move this period to just after the "Isaiah (sic)" quotation and take the first three verses of Mark to be the introduction to his persuasive discourse. Finally, we will add the verb "to be" just after the introduction to the quotation, which will make the messenger prophecy "(The) guiding principle of the gospel of Jesus Christ Son of God."

6. Caurie Beaver, *Mark: A Twice-Told Tale* (Xlibris Corporation, 2004), pp. 75–79.

Arché as the Chronological Beginning of the Gospel Story

If we are to make a case for taking the first word of Mark (arché) as the logical starting-point of the gospel of Mark, we must first explain why it has for so long been considered the chronological beginning of that gospel. As Mark was translated into the English language, the first word of the gospel (arché) was rendered as "(the) beginning" of the gospel story. Because Mark's first interpreters, Matthew and Luke, converted Mark's topical order into a chronological sequence, Mark's gospel has from the first century been read as a story, the gospel story. Since a story required a chronological starting-point, arché was understood as its temporal beginning. In the eighteenth and nineteenth centuries historians came to view Mark as a historical or biographical account, which also required a chronological beginning. With the shift from a historical to a literary study of Mark, there was no change in the meaning assigned to arché because even a fictional story required a chronological beginning.

However, problems arose when scholars attempted to specify the exact point of this beginning. According to Elaine Pagels, "Mark opens his gospel by telling of Jesus' baptism. . ."[7] This oversight is pardonable because her very excellent book is not primarily about the gospel of Mark. Mark's gospel does not begin with the baptism of Jesus; it begins with an announcement of the gospel and an appeal to prophecy. The Scholars Bible translation of Mark acknowledged the messenger prophecy as the beginning of the gospel, "The good news of Jesus the anointed begins with something Isaiah
    the prophet wrote:"[8]

---

7. Elaine Pagels, *Beyond Belief* (New York: Vintage Books, A Divisions of Random House Inc., 2003), p. 26.

8. Daryl D. Schmidt, *The Gospel of Mark*, The Scholars Bible (Sonoma, California, Polebridge Press, 1990), p. 43.

Conclusion

In order to accomplish this feat the translator was obliged to change a Greek noun, "beginning (arché)" into a verb "begins".

Another commentator who interpreted the first word of Mark, arché, chronologically, felt compelled to link verse one to verse four in which John's story began. He considered the intervening prophecy of verses two and three parenthetical. This is clearly revealed in his proposed translation of Mark 1:1-4.

"The starting-point of the Good News about Jesus Christ (in accordance with the scriptural words of the Prophet Isaiah, "The voice of a man crying in the desert, 'Make ye ready the way of the Lord, Make straight his paths.'"), was John, who baptized in the desert, and proclaimed a baptism of repentance with a view to remission of sins."

By placing the verb "to be" after the prophecy and a period after verse four, Rawlinson created a long sentence in which the prophecy is treated as a parenthesis. In an apparent effort to reduce the size of the parenthetical element to make it more acceptable this translation omitted Mark 1: 2b,

Behold, I send my messenger before thy face, who shall prepare thy way;[9]

Another consequence of interpreting arché as the beginning of a story is the tendency to extend the introduction so as to incorporate as many of the story elements as possible. The arrangement of the Greek text of Mark by Westcott and Hort suggested that Mark's introduction extended only through verse eight. R.H. Lightfoot and James M. Robinson expanded Mark's introduction through verse thirteen.[10] Others suggested that Mark's introduction ended at verse fifteen.[11] This enlarged introduction accurately

---

9. A. E. J. Rawlinson, *St. Mark* (London: Metheun & Co. LTD. 36 Essex Street W.C., 1925), p. 6.

10. R. H. Lightfoot, *The Gospel Message of St. Mark* (Eugene, Oregon: Wipf and Stock Publishers, 1950), p. 15. James M. Robinson, *The Problem of History in Mark and Other Essays* Philadelphia: Fortress Press, 1982), p. 70, Note 1.

11. M. Eugene Boring, "Mk. 1:1-15 And the Beginning of the Gospel" *Semeia 52 How Gospels Begin* (Society of Biblical Literature, 1991), p. 55.

reflected the underlying story in Mark, but did not adequately account for the persuasive discourse that framed the gospel.

When I wrote my book, *Mark A Twice-Told Tale*, I treated Mark as a story. That is why I utilized the parable of the Vineyard to cast light on the gospel's story elements, since the parable recapitulated so much of the gospel story. However, such a choice also ignored the persuasive discourse that dominated the gospel.[12] A better choice would have been the messenger prophecy. In fact I did show how elements of the prophecy, such as the desert, the way etc., extended throughout the gospel in such a way as to virtually generate its structure. However, my conception of the messenger prophecy as a passion prophecy prevented me from then realizing the full significance of its role in ordering the Markan discourse.

It will be seen that my choice of the messenger prophecy as the text of Mark's persuasive discourse is in line with the practice of Robinson and other scholars of choosing a short passage in Mark by which to reveal the meaning of the gospel. In my book I attributed this procedure to the undue influence of the pulpit on the study.[13] However, since the study of rhetoric saturated Mark's environment, his use of a text in the preacher's sense of a short passage in order to launch his "sermon" may have been due to the influence of the ancient *pulpit or lectern*.

Another question deserves at least a brief mention: Why have Bible translators not resorted to the logical meaning of arché? In the first place many "translations" are revisions of the King James Version, which is, itself, a revision of earlier translations. Recent revisers' two main concerns were to correct the manuscript base and to update the language where words had changed their meaning. An example of the second concern is the word gospel, whose meaning is no longer common knowledge, being replaced by the translation "good news." Also Holy Ghost is now translated as Holy Spirit. In the case of "beginning" the meaning of the word remained the same from King James' day until now; it was just not the best translation in the first place. Even in the case of a modern

12. Caurie Beaver, *Mark A Twice-Told Tale*, p. 45f.
13. Caurie Beaver, *Mark: A Twice-Told Tale*, p. 35f.

"translation" such as Goodspeed's New Testament, which rearranged the books in chronological order beginning with I Thessalonians, and is touted to be a new translation, the influence of the King James Version and its revisers is discernable.

Arché as the Guiding Principle of a Persuasive Discourse

The *guiding principle* of the good news of Jesus Christ, the Son of God, as it is written in the prophet Isaiah, *is as follows*:

> "See, I am sending my messenger ahead of you,
> who will prepare your way;
> the voice of one crying out in the wilderness:
> 'Prepare the way of the Lord,
> make his paths straight.'"
> (Mk. 1: 1–3, RSV).

Using The New Oxford Annotated Bible, I have made only necessary changes: arché is translated as "The guiding principle" instead of "The beginning", after "the Son of God" I placed a comma instead of a period, and after "make his paths straight I placed a period instead of a comma. Finally, I added the words "is as follows" after "the prophet Isaiah," creating a complete sentence in which "The guiding principle" is the subject and the messenger prophecy is the predicate.

Interpretation through Punctuation

Since the Greek manuscripts of Mark contain no punctuation, the addition of periods and commas etc. is an act of interpretation. In regard to the passage in question there is considerable disagreement as to how it is to be punctuated. The most important choice has to do with the placement of the period because it indicates the extent of the sentence. I have chosen to place the period after verse three and consider the first three verses the introduction of Mark, not the introduction of the gospel story, but the prooemium of a persuasive discourse.

Those who place the period after verse one usually consider it the title of the gospel. Some have even gone so far as to suggest that arché, beginning, was added later converting the Greek word for gospel from a nominative to a genitive. Originally it would have simply read "The Gospel of Jesus Christ" instead of "The Beginning of the Gospel of Jesus Christ."[14] My solution does not require such a speculative reconstruction of the text.

Finally, before the messenger prophecy I have chosen to place the words "as follows" instead of a colon[15] to make the meaning more explicit. The variety of punctuation used elsewhere in the passage affects its meaning less than the above instances. Of course, I reject the notion that the messenger prophecy is parenthetical.

To Be or Not to Be: The Omission of the Verb "To Be" in the Greek Sentence.

Nigel Turner points out that it was a fairly common practice in constructing the Greek sentence to omit the verb "to be", which was viewed as a weak copula that could easily be supplied. After conceding that it made good sense to add the verb "to be" to the first three verses of Mark, he decided against it on purely statistical grounds.[16] In my opinion by translating arché as "guiding principle" instead of "beginning", the addition of the verb "to be" to the passage once again becomes a viable option.

---

14. C. E. B. Cranfield, *The Gospel According to St. Mark* (Cambridge: Cambridge University Press, 1959), p. 34.

15. Robert A. Guelich, *Mark 1–8:26* Word Biblical Commentary, Vol. 34A, (Dallas, Texas Word Book Publishers, 1989), p. 6.

16. Nigel Turner, Grammatical Insights into the New Testament (New York: T&T Clark International A Continuum imprint, 2004), pp. 27–28.

Conclusion

Arché as a Guiding Principle

By far the most important change I have made in this passage is to translate the Greek word arché as "guiding principle". Although it remains a minority opinion, there is some support for it. While a few authors have recognized that "governing principle" or "rule" etc. is a possible translation of arché, no one, to my knowledge has systematically drawn the implications of doing so. They continue to operate with the translation "beginning," which has strong chronological connotations, and even confuse it with the term "rule," which carries the alternate logical meaning. Witness this fusion or confusion of the two meanings in the following quotation from a recent commentary.

> *The beginning*: In Greek *arch*é can mean "starting point, foundation, origin," and even "rule," or "governing principle." The meaning in Mark 1:1 is linked to whether a period or a comma is placed after "Son of God." In the former case v. 1 is a kind of title or *incipit* to the whole work, whereas in the latter case the beginning is in the fulfillment of the prophecy quoted in vv.2–3 ("The beginning . . . as it is written . . ."). Our translation interprets v. 1 as a title for the whole work, so that the faith and proclamation of Mark's community have both their "beginning" and "rule" of interpretation in the story of Jesus about to unfold.[17]

From this quotation it is clear that punctuation and interpretation go hand in hand. It is also clear that their preference for the chronological term "beginning" is conditioned by their understanding of Mark as ". . . the story of Jesus about to unfold." Even so they are reluctant to give up completely the benefits conferred by the term bearing the logical meaning, so they opt for a coordination of the two terms "beginning" and "rule".

Ernest Best in his book *Mark The Gospel As Story* also attempts to have it both ways.

17. John R. Donahue, S.J., and Daniel J. Harrington, S.J., *The Gospel of Mark, Sacra Pagina Series, v. 2* (Collegeville, Minnesota: A Michael Glazier Book, The Liturgical Press, 2002), pp. 59–60.

> That the book however is a verbal statement of the gospel is true whether we understand 'the beginning' in v. 1. To refer either to John the Baptizer (vv. 2–8), to the Prologue (vv. 2–13 or vv. 2–15), to the earthly life of Jesus as the beginning of the Christian movement, or give the word the meaning 'origin' or 'principle'.[18]

He lays all of these choices alongside one another as if the "verbal statement of the gospel" would remain the same regardless of which alternative one chose. We will soon see what a difference it makes.

> A final attempt to combine the two terms is found in a "popular" work on Mark. Indeed, Mark alone begins with a reference to the 'beginning' or 'first principle', and then an expounding of 'the way of the Lord' in line with the Solomonic wisdom in Proverbs addressed to the son."[19]

Did he forget John 1:1? "In the beginning (arché) was the word . . ." While Horne linked the 'beginning' or 'first principle' with one element of the prophecy that followed, "the way of the Lord," he did not relate it to the other themes of the prophecy which appear throughout Mark: the desert, the messenger, and the Lord. When we include all of these elements, we see the connection not only between "the guiding principle" and the prophecy but also between the prophecy and the rest of the gospel. Just as the messenger prepared the way of the Lord in the prophecy, John prepared the way of Jesus in the gospel. Finally, Willi Marxsen paved the way for the logical translation of arché as guiding principle rather than chronological beginning by observing that the connection between events in Mark was not temporal but topical. Writing about the different blocks of material on "Jesus—the Baptist—the Old Testament", Marxsen claimed,

---

18. Ernest Best, *Mark The Gospel As Story* (Edinburgh T&T Clark 59 George Street, 1983, Reprinted 1988), p. 38.

19. Mark Horne, *The Victory According to Mark* (Moscow, ID: Canon Press, 2003), p. 43.

Conclusion

The connection is topical, that is, it is made from a theological or, strictly speaking, Christological point of view."[20]

If I understand his comment on the term arché, Marxsen preferred the logical to the chronological meaning of the word. Concerning this term he wrote,

> "The word arché here, as elsewhere in Mark, does not mark a point of departure for a development in sequence, but rather the starting point to which a given datum can be traced."[21]

By his use of such terms as "beginning", "earliest point", and "present facts" Walter Wink in his paraphrase of Marxsen tends to soften the latter's rejection of the temporal sense of arché. Wink "translated" Marxsen's sentence, as follows,

> "The 'beginning' is not just the point of departure for Mark's Gospel but even more the earliest point back to which present facts can be traced in order to display their meaning."[22]

The Prophecy as the Principle

My only problem with Marxsen's view is that it does not specify exactly what the "guiding principle" (arché) was and how it operated in Mark's argument. Before we attempt to correct this omission, it may help to discuss the translation of this key term. In the English language we express the logical sense of arché with the Latin derived word "principle". "Beginning" has too much of a chronological connotation to be used here. If we had used the Greek term instead, the title of William James' *Principles of Psychology* would have been called the Archai of Psychology. The

---

20. Willi Marxsen, *Mark the Evangelist*, Translated by James Boyce, Donald Juel, and William Poehlmann (Nashville: Abingdon Press, 1969), p. 42.

21. Ibid.

22. Walter Wink, *John the Baptist in the Gospel Tradition* (Eugene, OR.: Wipf and Stock Publishers, 2000), p. 5.

Greek term is found in such words as archaeology, and archaic etc. There are several ways to express the logical sense of the Greek word arché: first principle, governing principle, guiding principle, organizing principle, fundamental notion or basic teaching etc. Even *beginning* or *starting point* are acceptable if they are taken in the logical sense.

It may even be significant that arché in Mark is singular, "guiding principle" and not plural, "basic principles." This leads us to look for a particular principle, which we find in the messenger prophecy. Therefore the first consequence of taking arché in the logical sense is to shift the beginning or starting point of the gospel from the activity of John the Baptist to the messenger prophecy, which can then be understood as the "guiding principle" of the gospel of Jesus Christ, Son of God.

By far the most important discussion of arché in Mark 1:1 is that of Allen Wikgren, one of the former editors of *The Greek New Testament*. After listing six different views of the first verse of Mark and discussing them briefly, he opted for considering the verse the title of the gospel of Mark. Then he called attention to the ambiguity of the current translation of the first word of Mark as "beginning," and suggested that an alternate translation might be more accurate.

After correctly translating arché as "first thing," without explanation he shifted from the singular to the plural. He claimed,

> . . .that arché in the Markan passage may mean 'first thing' in the sense of 'rudiments' or 'elements' or 'essentials' of the gospel.[23]

This is the closest Wikgren comes to actually translating the "title" of Mark. If he had consistently translated arché as a singular, he might have found his "first thing" (principle) in the messenger prophecy. In his discussion of the parallels in Hebrews 5:12 and 6:1 he adhered to the singular in his (Goodspeed's) translation of arché: Heb. 5:12, "the very elements of Christian truth," and Heb. 6:1,

---

23. Allen Wikgren, "ΑΡΧΗ ΤΟΥ ΕΥΑΓΓΕΛΙΟΥ" *Journal of Biblical Literature*, 61 (1942), 17.

"leaving elementary Christian teaching."[24] Of course the use of the term "Christian" is an anachronism because neither Hebrews nor Mark contain the word Christian.

If these parallels in Hebrews indicate that its author was acquainted with Mark, then he probably considered Mark the elementary instruction and his own work the more advanced teaching. Wikgren appeared to have endorsed such a view.[25] However, that was not Mark's view of his own work because his gospel contains both levels of meaning: the parable for outsiders and the interpretation for insiders.

When Wikgren objected to supplying the verb "to be," *estin*, in order to connect arché with the messenger prophecy, he may have inadvertently involved himself in a contradiction. He claimed that one could reasonably expect a scribe to have supplied the verb "to be" if it were implied, and none did. On the other hand in regard to Mark 13:8 he wrote,

> This is but the beginning of the birthpangs. This is a statement with a subject and a predicate in which it is imperative that the verb be supplied.[26]

How much more it would have been incumbent upon a scribe to have added the verb "to be" in this case, and yet Wikgren did not even bother to inquire as to whether one did. His assumption that the verb "to be" should be placed before the introduction to the prophecy rather than after it is problematic. Finally, his hypothetical expectation that

> . . .some scribe would yield to the insistent call for an inferential particle in verse 4. 'The beginning of the gospel . . . (was) as was prophesied. . ., (for) John came, etc.'[27]

was a direct consequence of Wikgren and *The Greek New Testament's* placement of a comma instead of a period after the prophecy.

24. *Ibid*. p. 18.
25. *Ibid*. p. 19.
26. *Ibid*. p. 13.
27. *Ibid*. p. 13.

The Principle as the Premise

Aristotle considered these principles, which were drawn from the opinions of great thinkers, past and present, as premises from which he could form syllogisms and by means of which he could construct a deductive science in order to make the subject in question intelligible. If we are to believe the masterful study of Aristotle by John Herman Randall Jr. making the world intelligible was what Aristotle's science was all about.[28]

In my book *Mark A Twice-Told Tale* I pointed out that Mark called the Forerunner and Messiah John and Jesus in the first half of the gospel and Elijah and the Son of Man in the second half. I compared this to the parable and its interpretation.[29] By observing certain rhetorical conventions adopted by Mark we may be able to be more specific about the origin of this pattern, and even shed light on the elusive search for that holy grail of Markan research, its genre.

If our translation of arché is correct, the gospel of Mark can be read as a syllogism writ large, in which the guiding principle contained in the messenger prophecy becomes its major premise. This syllogism, which formed the backbone of the gospel's structure, can be displayed graphically as follows:

> Major Premise: God sent his messenger to prepare the way of the Lord in the desert.
> Minor Premise: John prepared the way of Jesus in the desert.
> Conclusion: Therefore, John was the messenger and Jesus is the Lord.

The major premise is identical with Mark's introduction (Mk. 1: 1–3). The elaboration of the minor premise comprises the first half of the gospel (Mk. 1: 4–8: 31). Since the minor premise cannot contain the conclusion, which identified John and Jesus as Elijah and the Son of Man, all Mark can do at this point is describe their

---

28. John Herman Randall Jr., *Aristotle* (New York: Columbia University Press, 1960), pp. 32f.

29. Caurie Beaver, *Mark A Twice-Told Tale*, pp. 107f.

respective activities and imply that they conform to the prophecy especially with regard to the order in which they appeared: John first and Jesus second. This view has obvious implications for the "secrecy" theme in Mark.

It was only in the middle of the gospel that Mark drew the conclusion that identified John as Elijah and Jesus as the Son of Man. Even here he did not do so explicitly, but rather by referring his auditors back to the messenger prophecy, "as it is written of him" and "how is it written". When Mark elaborated the conclusion of the syllogism in the second half of the gospel, he linked the death of John the Baptist, which he had described previously, with that of the Son of Man. The conclusion included Jesus predictions of his death and resurrection "on the way".

Finally, in another tightly reasoned enthymeme, Mark's Jesus identified the Messiah as David's Lord and not his son (Mk. 12: 35–37). In her book *Sowing the Gospel*, Mary Ann Tolbert discussed the above enthymeme and others.[30] An enthymeme is a shortened form of a syllogism used in public speaking in which the speaker omitted the premises that he shared with the audience, usually culturally conditioned and deeply held beliefs. In order to bring to light these hidden premises, Tolbert exhibited the full syllogistic form of Mark's / Jesus' argument. In an appendix to my first book I discussed at length the enthymeme about the Davidic descent of the Messiah.[31]

Arché Elsewhere in Mark

It is worthwhile to ask whether Mark used the term arché elsewhere in the gospel in the logical sense. He used arché three other times: Mk. 10: 6, and 13: 8 and 9. In the last two references the temporal element *may* predominate: The second reference (Mk. 13: 8) referred to the beginning of the tribulation period and the third one (Mk. 13: 9) to the time since the beginning of creation.

---

30. Mary Ann Tolbert, *Sowing the Gospel* (Minneapolis: Fortress Press, 1960), pp. 32f.

31. Caurie Beaver, *Mark: A Twice-Told Tale*, pp. 209–216.

However, in the first reference (Mk. 10: 6) the context would suggest that a non-temporal or logical meaning was primarily intended. In a complex argument about divorce Mark had Jesus appeal to God's creation as the basis of his reasoning. The poetic version in Genesis is frequently used in the marriage ceremony, but Mark's Jesus used it in a reasoned argument about the permissibility of divorce. The Pharisees had just challenged Jesus with the question as to whether it was lawful for a man to put away (divorce) his wife. Jesus in turn asked them what Moses *commanded*. They replied that Moses *permitted* divorce by a bill of divorcement. Jesus then argued that Moses *allowed* divorce because of the hardness of their hearts, but maintained that the original intention of creation was otherwise.

Arché in the Book of Hebrews

Since the view of Mark as a persuasive discourse brings that gospel closer to Hebrews, the other theological essay, sermon, or to use the author's own term, a word of exhortation, it should not be surprising to find parallels in that work to Mark's use of arché to mean principle. Hebrews was already considered a reasoned discourse as opposed to a story, so the chronological meaning of arché, beginning, was not even considered. Hagner translated Hebrews 6:1 as "The 'elementary teachings (sic) about Christ'", or "Literally, the 'beginning of the word of Christ' . . ." However, "beginning" is not the literal meaning of arché, but simply an alternate meaning of the word.[32] We now have a book that discusses the relationship between the story and persuasive discourse in the book of Hebrews. In his book *Understanding the Book of Hebrews* Kenneth Schenck writes about *The Story Behind The Sermon*, the subtitle of his work. In it he lumped the gospels together and compared them to Hebrews.

---

32. Donald A. Hagner, *Encountering the Book of Hebrews* (Grand Rapids, Michigan: Baker Academic, a division of Baker Book House Company, 2004), p. 86.

Conclusion

"Thus while a Gospel is a 'story-as-discoursed' in a narrative, Paul's letters and Hebrews are 'stories-as-discoursed' in rhetoric."[33]

He apparently still considered the gospels as primarily narratives or stories.

The parallels to Mark 1:1 found in Hebrews 5:12 and 6:1 have not gone unnoticed.[34] They are clearer in Greek.

> Αρχη του ευαγγελιου Ἰησου Χριστου [νιου θεου].
> The guiding principle of the gospel of Jesus Christ, the Son of God. (Mk. 1:1).

> τα στοιχεια τηζ αρχηζ των λογιων του θεου
> The basic elements of the oracles of God. (Heb. 5:12)

> . . . τον τηζ αρχηζ του Χριστου λογον . . .
> . . . the basic teaching about Christ . . . (Heb. 6:1)

Is it possible that the author of Hebrews is here alluding to the first verse of Mark? Notice that the singular of arché is used in all three quotations.

Mark portrayed Jesus' disciples as lacking understanding; the author of Hebrews chided his addressees for being dull of understanding (Heb. 5:1). He said they ought to be teachers, but instead need to be taught "The basic elements of the oracles of God" (Heb. 5:12). They should be on a meat diet, but, as babes in Christ, they are still on a milk diet. Then, astonishingly, the writer of Hebrews urged his readers / hearers to leave the basic teaching about Christ and go on to perfection. The teaching that the author of Hebrews urged his readers / auditors to abandon on their journey to perfection comprised the common "Christian" teachings: repentance from dead works, faith toward God, baptisms, laying on of hands,

---

33. Kenneth Schenck, *Understanding Hebrews: The Story Behind the Sermon* (Louisville, Kentucky: Westminster John Knox Press, 2003), p. 111 n. 9.

34. C. E. B. Cranfield, *The Gospel According to Mark*, p. 34.

resurrection from the dead and eternal judgment, which are also found in the gospel of Mark.

In the introduction to Hebrews (Heb. 1: 1–5) there are other parallels to the parable of the Vineyard in Mark (Mk. 12: 1–12). Again, agreement may have been mediated through a common tradition. Both Hebrews and the parable have

1. a succession of prophets through whom God spoke in the past,
2. a revelation in the last days,
3. through God's Son,
4. who is the heir, and
5. both refer to Psalm 2:7 near the beginning of their discourse.

At a minimum I would like to suggest that Hebrews looked back to a work or works like Mark, as the foundation of the gospel, a work comprised of basic or elementary teachings. The author of Hebrews not only urged his addressees to forsake these elementary teachings, but also claimed that to return to them was to crucify the Son of God again (Heb. 6:6).

The more advanced teachings were, of course, those found in his own work, which taught that Jesus was the Son of God and a High Priest after the order of Melchizedek, who offered himself as a perfect sacrifice replacing the repeated sacrifices of the "Old Testament". The author of Hebrews even claimed that once a person had become enlightened and fell away, he could not be restored through repentance, the essential part of the "elementary" teaching mentioned above. The one time repentance advocated by Hebrews corresponded to the once and for all sacrifice of Jesus. To allow a second repentance after lapsing would be to teach multiple sacrifices like those under the law, except that the sacrifice in this case would be the sacrifice or crucifixion of the Son of God again, which would be to deny that Jesus's once for all sacrifice was sufficient.

We have found parallels between the content of Hebrews' introduction (Heb. 1: 1–5), and the Parable of the Vineyard (Mk. 12:

1–12). As for the form and function of Hebrews' introduction, it constituted the prooemium or rhetorical introduction to the following persuasive discourse.[35] In this role, that is, as regards its form, it is parallel to Mark 1: 1–3, the prooemium of the gospel of Mark.

Conclusion

For almost two thousand years the gospels have been taken to be primarily stories. According to John Drury, this trait accounts for their tremendous hold on our imagination:

> Stories (to use a term which deliberately begs the question of fact or fiction) communicate doctrines to the ordinary man more vividly than abstract schemes or moral advice because they are more concrete and more fun.[36]

We find it much easier to locate ourselves in the stories than to determine the points made by them in their original setting. Therefore, we strip away the argumentative framework of the stories and use them as mirrors to reflect our own concerns.

When I wrote my book *Mark A Twice-Told Tale*, I was under the influence of William Beardslee's contrast between Aristotle's poetics and rhetoric. Following Beardslee's advice I used Aristotle's poetics in combination with modern literary criticism to study Mark. Since Mark contains stories and an overriding plot, it is still valid to study the gospel of Mark in this way. Actually, the materials in Mark are suggestive of two different genres: On the one hand we have narratives or stories and on the other hand preaching or a persuasive discourse, just as light may be viewed as waves or particles. However, it is doubtful that the narrative is primary in Mark because it has not been able to accommodate the argumentative and persuasive elements in the gospel. Nor has it led to a determination of the gospel's genre.

---

35. Victor C. Pfitzer, *Hebrews* (Nashville: Abingdon Press, 1997), p. 22.

36. John Drury, *Tradition and Design in Luke's Gospel: A Study in Early Christian Historiography* (Atlanta: John Knox Press, 1977), p. 1.

On the other hand when we begin with the persuasive elements in Mark, rhetorical analysis can easily accommodate the story elements. It will be seen that Mark began with a conventional prooemium or introduction whose points are illustrated and elaborated in the narrative that followed. The frequent practice of scholars, such as James Robinson, of interpreting Mark through the lens of a single passage is based on a correct intuition. In my book *Mark A Twice-Told Tale*, I demonstrated a connection between the messenger prophecy and the rest of the gospel. However, I then viewed the messenger prophecy as a passion prophecy.[37] It is now clear to me that it is much more than that. Like preachers today Mark chose a text, the messenger prophecy, which generated the structure of his persuasive discourse.

---

37. Caurie Beaver, *Mark: A Twice-Told Tale*, pp. 65–85.

www.ingramcontent.com/pod-product-compliance
Lightning Source LLC
Chambersburg PA
CBHW071505150426
43191CB00009B/1428